Called to Be Human

Called to Be Human

Letters to My Children
on Living a Christian Life

Michael Jinkins

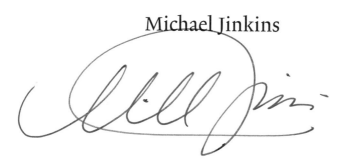

William B. Eerdmans Publishing Company

Grand Rapids, Michigan / Cambridge, U.K.

Published 2009 by
Wm. B. Eerdmans Publishing Co.
2140 Oak Industrial Drive N. E., Grand Rapids, Michigan 49505 /
P. O. Box 163, Cambridge CB3 9PU U. K.

Printed in the United States of America

14 13 12 11 10 09   7 6 5 4 3 2 1

Library of Congress Cataloging-in-Publication Data

Jinkins, Michael, 1953-
Called to be human: letters to my children on living a Christian life /
Michael Jinkins.
p.   cm.
ISBN 978-0-8028-6300-3 (alk. paper)
1. Christianity. 2. Christian life.   I. Title.

BR123.J55 2009
248.4 — dc22
2009006927

www.eerdmans.com

For Jeremy, Jessica,
Caroline & Cliff

Contents

Why I Wrote This Book

Young adults ask Big Questions. Does life have meaning and purpose? If so, is it just the meaning and purpose I bring to it, or is there something or someone else who gives life its meaning and purpose? Often they ask these questions in personal terms: What is the purpose of my life? What can I believe in? How should I invest my life? Mostly these questions come in plain brown wrappers.

During the summer of 2006, the *Chronicle of Higher Education* published an article that reported on surveys of thousands of American college students. The studies the article describes reinforce what many educators and parents already know: as young people bridge into adulthood, they want to find times when and places where and persons with whom they can explore their Big Questions.[1]

This book addresses some of the Big Questions that young adults are asking, and it does so through a series of letters to the two young adults who are closest to me, my children. I have written this book for them, for other young adults, and for their parents, teachers, pastors, and mentors. I hope we in these latter groups can encourage our young people to freely and fearlessly interrogate the universe they live in. The biggest questions get bigger, and the answers are worth the search.

THE LETTERS

A Letter to Everyone Else

Dear friends,

We are often told these days that people prefer to describe themselves as "spiritual, not religious." And we have long been told that many people object to identifying themselves with "organized religion."

After considerable reflection, I have come to realize I am not very religious myself. (You'll learn more about what I mean by this in the letters that follow.) And because I don't really understand what the word *spiritual* means today — given the fact that it seems to mean something different for every person who uses the term — I'm not sure I would describe myself as spiritual either. I am, however, a person of faith.

Faith is a matter of trust and reverence more than it is a matter of beliefs and belief systems. This is not to say that beliefs are irrelevant. It matters a great deal whom you trust and what you hold sacred. But the older I get, the more I see that life is mystery and the less certainty I possess. I take more of life on faith. I *trust* a lot more than I *know*. So my beliefs have become increasingly modest in their claims while they have become more extravagant in their hopes.

I hope, for example, that at the creative heart of this universe there is goodness. I know there's freedom in the universe. Anyone who pays any attention to the messiness of life knows there is freedom. And I value this freedom, because life would not be worthwhile without it. But I hope there's goodness too.

Faith, hope, and love: these are personal issues. I trust. I hope. And I trust and hope because against all odds I love.

Love is the biggest risk of human existence. Pascal tossed the dice and sweated his wager for the sake of salvation: even though God's existence cannot be proven by reason, we should nevertheless wager that God exists because by so doing we have nothing to lose and everything to gain.[1] Good for him! But this is my wager: In the face of a universe about which we know next to nothing (*really*, we know next to nothing about this universe we so blithely take for granted), and in the teeth of a life littered with wonder (I love novelist Marilynne Robinson's recent comment: "We are living through something that would make any miracle seem commonplace."[2]), and in spite of the obvious perils and terrors that are woven into every twisted fiber of this world in which we live and move and have our being, I trust that love is behind it all, that love upholds it all, that love makes it all worthwhile in the end, though I know from bitter experience that to love is to grieve, if not today, then someday soon.

This brings me to the subject of this book, and the reason I am beginning by writing a letter to you, the reader: I hardly knew the character of faith, the scale of hope, and the risk of love until I became a parent. There is nothing that connects us so directly to the Creator's unimaginable vulnerability — creating an entire universe that is both loved and free — like bringing children into the world. Love lay like a pale promise on the page of some admired but largely unintelligible book until I loved these two persons to whom the letters in this book are written. Trust remained an abstract concept and hope was the domain of pie-in-the-sky optimists until I risked my soul in loving them.

The book you now hold in your hands began as a project called *Letters to New Christians,* but that book never really worked. At least, I could not write it. Then it became *Letters to Young Christians.* Yet try as I might, the letters in that book were not real enough to speak to the spiritual needs of youth and young adults. In order for this to be a book for anyone else's children, it first had to be a book for my own children. It took more than two years and at least three trashed drafts of this book to realize that what I had to write in these letters is a testament of my faith, bearing witness to my children, in the hope that what I write to them may be of some interest and value to others.

Having said this, however, I must hasten to say that if these letters are of value it is not because our experience, the experience of our family, is exceptional, but because it is so ordinary and commonplace. What we feel and know is simply what parents and sons and daughters and brothers and sisters feel and know. Our frequent blind spots are as unexceptional as are our occasional insights. This is as obvious when it comes to reflecting on our personal foibles as it is when we reflect on our faith.

While I am a theologian by education and a minister by vocation, I do not believe that bearing witness to our children is a "professional" activity. It is something we are called to do as parents. Witness-bearing is part of the vocation of parenthood, not least because parenthood calls us to bear witness to the Creator and divine Parent, whose unfathomable mystery lies, as one theologian puts it, in the fact that God exists solely in dispensing himself, "a flowing wellspring with no holding-trough beneath it."[3] In other words, our bearing witness as parents holds our parenting accountable to the God who is love while it reminds us and our children of our calling to follow Jesus of Nazareth, in whom we believe God is revealed.

Ultimately, it is simply impossible not to bear witness, whether intentionally or unintentionally. For instance, we tell our children what matters most to us in all sorts of ways: by how we spend time and money; by what we talk about and what we avoid talking about; by how well we respect others, by the enemies we make and by who our friends are; by what we enjoy and at what we are outraged; by the quality of reverence we demonstrate and by the objects of our irreverence. At times we may bear witness eloquently. At times we may be tongue-tied. Sometimes we perform this task well, sometimes poorly. But there's no avoiding bearing witness. What varies is the level of intention we bring to the task. Because it's inevitable, bearing witness deserves some thought. And the way I have been thinking about it is by writing these letters to Jeremy and Jessica, two young adults, both very much on their own.

My children and I have passed through many stages together, from their infancy to their adulthood, and now we are friends. In those years, there were times when they were more dependent on their parents and times when they needed almost nothing at all from us — almost.

Generally speaking, parenting is more like coaching a team than quarterbacking one. You stand, largely helpless, on the sidelines in some of the biggest plays of the game. Sometimes the best coaching occurs in the locker room before the game or at halftime when plays are planned and miscues reviewed. Sometimes a lifted eyebrow is all that is needed to communicate disapproval, but often encouragement is the best remedy. My wife, Deborah, has always been a better coach than I am — mostly I just try not to throw chairs at the referees, though sometimes it's hard to resist. And, in retrospect, I am painfully aware of how often I misread the game.

I watch in awe the spectacle of my children's lives, and I wonder. Awe and wonder are, I believe, where every story of faith starts. Thus the great Jewish thinker Abraham Heschel says that the awareness of the ineffable is that with which our search must begin.[4] Where this story ends is well beyond our range of vision.

Faith is contagious. We catch it from others. Grandparents can be especially good carriers of the contagion. Many parents, friends, and teachers are carriers too. I suspect that one reason you are reading this book is because you wonder if you carry the bug, or if you can spread it.

I began by noting that many people don't want to be called religious anymore. Some people lament this fact. I'm not sure I do. Maybe what we are being told about "the problem with religion" today is not all that different from Søren Kierkegaard's problem with the established state religion — "Christendom," as he called it — in his native Denmark more than a hundred years ago. Kierkegaard basically said that Christendom was inoculating people with just enough of the dead virus of religion that they were unlikely ever to catch a living Christian faith.[5] If this is the point that people are trying to make by disowning the word "religious," then I do not lament the demise of religion, organized or otherwise, because anything that gets in the way of what God is up to in this wondrous creation isn't worth our time.

Jesus said that the truth will set us free. Someone else has added, however, that first the truth may make us miserable, or at least really uncomfortable. And anyone who has ever caught the real bug of faith knows this is true.

Letters to My Children

Dear Jeremy and Jessica,

One temptation in writing these letters to you is to try to ease into them slowly, to test the water with my big toe before wading in and tentatively paddling out, but I'm going to resist this temptation. Both of you are already swimming at the deep end of the pool, so I'm plunging in where you are by responding to a question you have both raised. *As Christians, what's the point of our faith?*

Jeremy, you raised this question with me a few years ago when you were taking courses in college in comparative religion and in Islam. Jessica, you asked me even more recently.

There are dozens of ways I could respond, but I think the best would be to come straight to the point: *The purpose of Christian faith is for us to become human.*

I'll put it even more bluntly. Christians believe that God became flesh and dwelt among us. And I do not for a moment think that God went to all the trouble of incarnation — becoming flesh — let alone the trouble of being crucified, just to make us religious. God became human to make human beings of us.

In fact, I would go so far as to say that religion is not one of God's big issues. I know there are lots of religious people. I just don't think God is religious. The Hebrew prophets, for example, talk about God's surprising lack of interest in matters religious. Listen to Micah 6:6-8: "With what shall I come to the Lord and bow myself before the God on high? Shall I come to him with burnt offerings, with yearling calves? Does the Lord take delight in thousands of rams, in ten thousand rivers of oil? Shall I present my first-born for my rebellious acts, the fruit of my body for the sin of my soul? The Lord has told you, O mortal, what is good; and what does the Lord require of you but to do justice, to love kindness, and to walk humbly with your God."

The prophet Amos tells of the God who's so angry about his people's behavior that he won't even attend their worship services anymore: "I hate, I reject your festivals, nor do I delight in your solemn assemblies. Even though you offer up to me burnt offerings and your grain offerings, I will not accept them; and I will not even look at the peace offerings of your fatlings. Take away from me the noise of your songs; I will not even listen to the sound of your harps. But let justice roll down like waters and righteousness like an ever-flowing stream."

The thing that stands out for me in these prophetic words is that God identifies religion as one of those things people do for all sorts of reasons — some good, some not so good. Yet God's interests run in another direction. God cares about justice and rightness, kindness and humility, mercy and goodness, working for peace and taking up the cause of those who don't have powerful friends in positions of influence. The priests might have been arguing over the quality and quantity of the incense used in the temple; God seems more incensed about what's happening in the streets just outside the building.

Often I get the feeling that people of faith confuse their interest in religion with reverence for God. As strange as it may seem, faith, trust, reverence toward God, and respect for other people are very different things from religion, which includes the collection of rituals, ceremonies, sacred procedures, and beliefs of our differing creeds. I've come to this conclusion after spending most of my adult life as a Christian theologian and a pastor.

I think God is playing for much bigger stakes than religion.

That's not to say that religion is not good. It can be. Religion can be a very good thing. But religion can also be very bad. And I share the concerns of some of my friends who don't believe in God, who avoid believing in God because they are afraid of religion and the destructive tendencies of some religious people. We have all seen cruelty and selfishness, sadism and violence, egotism and tyranny, all dressed up for church.

There are few things in this world more dangerous than a religious zealot who believes sincerely that he speaks and acts on behalf of God. There were crosses enough littering the ancient Roman Empire, concentration camps enough strewn across Nazi-occupied Europe, killing fields enough hidden beneath Southeast Asian turf, and smoldering rubble enough lying in downtown New York City to bear witness for all time to our relentless capacity to pervert our highest aspirations, whether religious or political, into the most deadly inhuman acts.

Repentance, like charity, begins at home. As a Christian and as a human being, it is utterly beyond my comprehension how a faith that reveres Jesus of Nazareth, executed by the brutal powers of this world, could ever allow itself to become the tool of such powers. But there it is. And here we are again.

So, this is my starting place. The place I choose to begin to bear witness to you, my children, whom I love more than life itself. I believe God wants us to become human. I believe that the whole point of the life, death, and resurrection of Jesus of Nazareth — as well as his teachings and ministry — is to make human beings of us.

I'll think more about what I mean when I say that God wants us to be human, and I'll try to unwrap these ideas as well as I can. At the very least I mean something similar to what Kurt Vonnegut meant in his novel *God Bless You, Mr. Rosewater* when he said, "Hello, babies. Welcome to Earth. It's hot in the summer and cold in the winter. It's round and wet and crowded. At the outside, babies, you've got about a hundred years here. There's only one rule that I know of, babies . . . you've got to be kind."[1]

I think it's a little more complicated than that. Vonnegut probably thought so too. But it's a good place to start, and I've been tempted many times to say precisely these words during a baptism.

There's just one thing more I want to say to both of you in this first letter, and it is a very personal word, perhaps a small confession in search of your absolution.

Most of our lives are lived in small publics. This is surely true for pastors and teachers like your parents, and for the people closest to them. We make anecdotes of our lives to communicate a point in the sermons we preach and the lessons we teach, the best of which are made at our own expense with self-effacement and with tongue in cheek. This fact is especially an occupational hazard for the people who are married to or are the children of pastors. A pastor recently reminded the seminary students in my class that Sunday morning comes round every 168 hours, and every pastor preaches on that schedule whether the Spirit moves her or whether the heavens are utterly silent. Living on that schedule, sometimes I have reached into the mixed bag of our lives as a family and pulled out something and crafted of it a story for the Sunday sermon trying to connect the good news of the gospel with the lives of the people in our congregation. I hope I have honored the gospel of Jesus Christ and respected you whenever I have done this. I say this now because writing these letters is a lot like writing a sermon.

A sermon should be a testament, if not a last will and testament, a rendering of accounts, saying a thing we are compelled to say because if we don't say that thing the stones themselves will cry out for the word to be heard. But, in some sense, our lives are like sermons too. This is, I think, why St. Paul refers to the members of the church at Corinth as a letter, written "with the Spirit of the living God." Letters, sermons, and wills, at their best, try to render an account, to bear witness, to tell the truth, the whole truth, and nothing but the truth.

We ought to be able to render an account of what we believe, what we truly believe, what we would be willing to die for, maybe more importantly what we would be willing to live for. I especially think a parent ought to be able to render such an account to his or her children.

This is what I'm going to do in the missives that follow. I am going to render to you an account of my faith, knowing that what I say to you is also being said in some small public beyond your hearing. Others, like neighbors gathered around the mailbox, will be reading your letters over your shoulders, but these letters really are your letters, and they really are from me, and I really mean what I am saying in them. They are as true as I know how to write them.

Dear Jessica,

On our way home from the art gallery, when I asked whether you'd be joining us for the Christmas Eve service this year at St. David's Church, you begged off. "God and I are having some issues right now, so I'd rather not come," you said.

I want you to know that my response to you then was not intended to be flippant, though it may have sounded that way at the time. If you remember, I said that God and I have been having an argument since before you were born, and that even if you and God are not getting along right now, we'd still like you to come with us to church on Christmas Eve. I meant this.

It's not abnormal in any real relationship for there to be stormy weather and seasons of calm. There have been times when I didn't even believe in the existence of God, and yet I felt compelled (in fact, I suspect I was compelled by God) to keep trying to talk to God, and to keep trying to listen for God. There have been other times when, despite the fact that I believed with absolute conviction in God's existence (and a great deal more), I didn't feel that God and I were on speaking terms at all.

I remember a conversation one day with one of my best friends in graduate school. We were shooting pool in the student rec room when he looked at me and said, "I long with all my heart to long for God again."

I took my shot, re-chalked the cue stick, paused, and said to him that it sounded to me like God and he might be in a pretty good place. Longing for the longing for God is not far from longing for God.

Doubt, conflict, tension, worry over the absence of joy and the empty feeling that God is not there, all of the various "nights of the soul" that haunt us waking and sleeping, our lament and anger at God's apparent distance in the midst of pain and sorrow and crisis, even disgust at the cynicism or the self-righteousness of God's disciples: these things are all aspects of faith. They are part and parcel of the struggle that represents faith's complicated topography.

Apathy, on the other hand: now, that's something that's opposed to faith. A lack of reverence for the holy and a lack of respect for humanity created in the image of God: these are faith's natural enemies. But a lively mind and heart engaged with God, fussing, feuding, and fuming with God over things that matter, even a life struggling mightily against God at certain moments: faith consists in such as this.

We can get such weird picture-book portraits of the saints of old. They almost become Zombies for Jesus, the walking dead in Christ, stalking stiff-legged from good work to good work with never a doubt. Few real saints look like that. Job argued with God. Jacob connived his way into a divine wrestling match. David made pretty nearly every mistake you can as a person and a king, but God loved to see him dance and gave his name to the Messiah. Real faith is a matter between living persons and a living God.

I appreciate reformer John Calvin's words: *In tota vita negotium cum Deo!* Okay, okay, I'll render that in the Queen's English. I like to translate the Latin like this: *In all of life we have our negotiations with God.* Negotiating all of life with God is what faith is all about.

There have been times in my life when the only thing that seemed to connect me to God was participation in the Lord's Supper. The act of receiving Communion felt like a cord, a tendril sometimes as thin as a strand in a spider's web, holding me in a tenuous relationship with God. I once mentioned this to a friend, much older and wiser. He said that one of the reasons the people of God come together to worship is to believe together. Some days we pray and believe on behalf of others who can't believe for themselves; some days they pray and believe on our behalf. But every day we can have this confidence: God always prays for us and believes on our behalf. Church is the place you go not because you have the faith to be there, but because you trust that someone else has the faith you need. Perhaps Doubting Thomas should be our patron saint. I've always felt he has gotten a bum rap.

"I believe; help my unbelief!" Maybe this is the truest prayer we can pray — that is, next to, "God, be merciful to me, a sinner."

Dear Jessica,

I take your point in response to my previous letter. What you're saying is not that you're having an argument with God (at least not right now). You just don't believe you have faith. Okay, I can buy that, but what do you mean by it? Frederick Buechner once observed, "Faith is better understood as a verb than as a noun, as a process than as a possession. It is on-again-off-again rather than once-for-all. Faith is not being sure where you're going but going anyway."[2]

I know there are people who believe that faith is about certainty; that faith is about being sure; that faith is even about proofs and evidence. There are people who treat faith like a possession, their very own private possession, something they are proud of having, something that entitles them to look down on those who don't have it. Some groups of Christians over the years — and even some today — have seemed to believe this. So have some members of other faiths. But George MacDonald, the Scottish mystic and writer, says in his classic fairy tale *The Princess and the Goblin,* "People must believe what they can, and those who believe more must not be hard upon those who believe less."[3] After all, none of us produced the faith we have.

If faith is a gift given by God (and MacDonald is simply reflecting a biblical perspective on this, by the way), then faith doesn't belong to us. We shouldn't brag about possessing faith. We can't conjure it up. We cannot hold on to it. We can't prevent it from departing. Faith doesn't bestow certainty on us. It didn't even bestow certainty on Jesus, and we believe Jesus is the "pioneer and perfecter" of our faith (Hebrews 12:2). Faith is "the assurance of things hoped for" (Hebrews 11:1). Faith is trust through and through, trust that makes hope substantial and real.

I take comfort in this. I also take comfort in the fact that while Jesus could see the outline of a cross in his future, even he didn't possess certainty about the road he traveled.

Jesus' prayer in the Garden of Gethsemane is a prayer of faith, not of certainty: "Father, for you all things are possible; remove this cup from me; yet, not what I want, but what you want." When Jesus prayed on the cross, "Father, into your hands I commend my spirit," this is faith in action. In both cases, Jesus didn't grasp a possession. Jesus didn't hold a certainty in his hand. He didn't have a hidden wild card up his sleeve. Jesus trusted that he was held by Another. Even if he couldn't clearly see what was ahead for him, especially if the road ahead looked suspiciously more like a precipitous drop from a cliff than a bend in the trail, he entrusted himself and the road he traveled and everything he didn't know to God, because he believed that God is faithful and good.

Do you remember that we had a conversation about this a long time ago? You were six years old, and it was on the night before you had open heart surgery. I know I will never forget that conversation. You, your mother, and I (and Jeremy too) had been on a roller-coaster ride of epic proportions for the month or so leading up to that moment. From the surprise diagnosis by your doctor, to the confirmation by the specialists at the hospital, finally to the scheduling of your operation: we were suffering from emotional and spiritual vertigo while trying to remain calm.

You had gotten ready for bed that night, and I was preparing to curl up on the cot the nurses had brought into your room for me to sleep on. I invited you to join me for my evening prayers before going to sleep. You prayed with me and had been quietly listening as I prayed from the *Book of Common Prayer* a prayer titled "For Those We Love." The prayer goes like this: "Almighty God, we entrust all who are dear to us to thy never-failing care and love, for this life and the life to come; knowing that thou art doing for them better things than we can desire or pray for; through Jesus Christ our Lord. Amen."

As soon as I finished this prayer, you reached over and squeezed my hand, and asked me, "Daddy, were you putting me in God's hands?"

I could hardly answer you for the knot in my throat. But I struggled to say, "Yes. Tomorrow when the doctors take you into surgery, I am entrusting you to God who loves you even more than I do (though I can't imagine how that's possible!). I trust God will do better things for you than I can desire or pray for."

I didn't know where that road would lead. I could not visualize what it would mean twenty-four hours later to stand next to you in the intensive care unit with you hooked up to a respirator and monitors and IVs and all sorts of other terrifying machines. I certainly couldn't imagine what it would mean to see you gradually return to health and eventually to possess health you had never known before. I just hoped, and the hope became a sort of solid trust, and the trust felt more like I was held than like something I was holding. It surely didn't feel like I knew for certain where the road would end. I didn't. I just trusted the One who walked with us. And I know — I know! — I didn't give myself that faith. Faith was given to me in a moment when I'm not sure I could have taken two more steps on my own.

Something similar happened when your mother had cancer a few years earlier. She and I realized in the middle of some very dark days, when you and Jeremy were very small, that no matter where that ordeal might lead, we could rest in God. I vividly remember driving her from the hospital after her surgery, both of us aware that more treatment — we didn't know what kind or how much — was still to come. We were both profoundly aware of a sense of calm, of peace, a restfulness that sustained us, as though we were relying on someone else's strength. I have no idea what it all meant, or where this trust came from. We didn't manufacture the faith we were given in that moment. We received it like hungry children grateful to return for second helpings.

God held us through your illness and your mother's, and has held us through a hundred, a thousand, other times of crisis, small and large. Faith has held us even when we didn't notice it. And then there are those moments when we did notice it, when our eyes opened and we saw the world with renewed wonder and joy, and we thought, "Ah, God."

These thoughts were on my mind yesterday when I was

teaching a theology class for a group of Southeast Asian church leaders. We were reading together Paul's Letter to the Romans where Paul seems almost to break into song — it reminds me of what they do in those old musicals you love to watch on late-night television, like *White Christmas,* when everyone is going about their business and then suddenly they start to sing and dance.

Paul has been slogging along in his letter to the Christians in Rome, trying to understand and explain God's continuing relationship with the people of Israel and God's new relationship with the Gentile world, and you sense that Paul is gaining new insights even as he is writing the letter. Then suddenly Paul just seems to break into song: "O the depth of the riches and wisdom and knowledge of God! How unsearchable are his judgments and how inscrutable his ways!" (Romans 11:33).

And I just had to pause for a moment in reading the passage and say to the students that maybe, just maybe, the most profound word Paul ever wrote in all his many letters, was that word *O* at the beginning of this exclamation of praise.

Dietrich Bonhoeffer says something to the effect that any real teaching about God begins in silence. I think there's truth in this, especially amid all the nonsense and gibberish and babble that passes for religious speech today. But I think it is even more true to say that any real word about God is inseparable from that utterance of amazement and awe that Paul expresses in the word *O.*

O — A circle, with nothing in the middle but air! That's how I think we live most truly by faith, sustained by the invisible hand of God in a vast creation that floats like down on the breath of God. A consciousness of our utter dependence on God hits us like a solid left hook to the solar plexus, and we wince with an audible, "O!" Or the beauty and majesty of life draws from our lungs our breath in a gust of unutterable admiration for what God can do and we gasp, "O!" So much faith is expressed in this circle of breath, this little O of exclamation at what God brings our way.

I have felt the extremes of this O in response to God in your company, hoping you would survive your childhood, then watching you thrive as a young woman; and in between these extremes I have become conscious of something about you and your quest for faith that I want you to know. It's articulated well in a beautiful, enigmatic passage I recently read by Abu Yazid al-Bistami, a Sufi master. He said: "This thing we tell of can never be found by seeking, yet only seekers find it."[4]

You, my daughter, are a seeker and a pilgrim by nature, and probably by vocation. I know you don't think you have faith right now. But I believe God has faith in you, and for you.

———

Dear Jeremy,

Our conversation today about your vocational future brought to mind something that happened not too long ago in a congregation here. I was their guest preacher that Sunday, and I preached a sermon titled "The Meaning of Life," in which I explored the question, *does God have a purpose for your life?* Immediately after worship a young man, a college freshman, asked if we could talk in the pastor's study. He reminded me a lot of you; like you, he was eager, intelligent, curious, and determined that his life should not just be spent, but that it be invested in something that matters.

Do you remember the talk you and I had many years ago as we were walking across the upper field at the farm in East Texas? We had been target shooting down by the pond. We were walking back toward the old house when for some reason, right out of the blue, you asked me, "Dad, did God talk to you?" I remember stopping in my tracks and asking you, "What do you mean, did God talk to me? When?" And you said, "You know, when God called you to be a minister, did God talk to you?" You must have been fifteen years old, certainly no more than that. It's been more than ten years.

I scrambled to put together a coherent response to your question. Finally I stammered something like, "Well, yes, Jeremy. God did speak to me. Yes. I sensed a deep, quiet motivation that God wanted my life for something other than what I had been planning."

You see, I had planned for as long as I could remember to become a lawyer just like my uncles Curtis and B. C. They were my heroes as a kid growing up in our small Southern town. Often when I was haunting my mother's office at City Hall, I'd wander a few doors down the block to Uncle Curtis's office across from the courthouse. I admired his quiet dignity, his wisdom, and I would sit in rapt silence listening to him, or just watching the traffic in and out of his office. I listened to stories that Uncle B. C. would tell about cases he was working on as eagerly as I watched Perry Mason on television. Probably my youthful aspirations were also shaped by the archetypal Southern lawyer of fiction, too, Atticus Finch in Harper Lee's *To Kill a Mockingbird*.

These were all powerful influences. I don't think I really ever questioned that my vocation would be the law (a profession I still respect, by the way). I thought I knew exactly where I was going.

But at the age of seventeen my life took an unexpected turn. My grandfather, your great-grandfather, died when I was twelve years old, and I drifted away from the church for a few years after that. Mother and Dad, your grandparents, stopped going for a while, too. Of course my grandmother, your great-grandmother, was always more than a pillar in the church, she was a pillar and load-bearing beam combined, and her quiet influence was there all along for all of us. But it was a high school friend who invited me back to church. At first I just played in the backup band for the big youth choir at his church. But I enjoyed the new friends I made there, and the music we made together. And within a few months gradually something came alive again in me, something I had forgotten about since my grandfather died.

My return to the church was, I suppose, a kind of "relapse" of Christian faith, when for a few years there I thought I had been cured of that disease forever. Music was an essential part of that return. My grandfather had been the choir director in our church, and he was a person of the most simple and personal faith I have ever known. He talked about "the Good Lord" with reverence and familiarity. We spent nearly every day of my childhood together, working, playing, talking, and always, *always,* singing.

Around this time, "God talked to me."

The conversation began when I began to experience some doubt about whether I really should become a lawyer: was I really "called" to be a lawyer, or was law just a profession I had decided on by default? Law is a great profession, and it can be a noble and sacred calling, but I began to wonder if it was *my* calling. I had simply assumed it would be, and had never really questioned it.

The doubt worked like an itch, just creating some vocational unease. Then I began to get these hints from other people that maybe I had another calling. God talks to us most of the time, I think, through other people, especially through voices in our church. God talked to me through people like my pastor, my Sunday school teachers, my youth director, my choir director, and my friends, all of whom asked me to take on leadership roles in the church — much to my surprise.

There were moments when I prayed alone, when I struggled with my Bible open before me, listening for the voice of God. I began to read the Gospels more carefully than ever before, and I was struck by the simplicity, the beauty, the power and original-ity of Jesus' message, and the distance between his claim on our lives and the conventional responses into which we had settled as a church. As a young man attempting to understand how I should respond faithfully to the Vietnam War, I remember being convicted by Jesus' Sermon on the Mount, Jesus' words, "You have heard that it was said, 'An eye for an eye, and a tooth for a tooth,' but I say to you, do not resist an evildoer. But if anyone strikes you on the right cheek, turn the other also" (Matthew 5:38-39). And as a young person trying to understand what it meant to be a Christian in a theologically conservative and deeply pious church, I was stung by his warnings against "prac-ticing your piety before others in order to be seen by them" (Mat-thew 6:1).

I was aware that my calling was suddenly up for grabs, that a vocational future I had believed to be long settled — I had hoped to go to Baylor University, Baylor Law School, do ROTC, gain a commission, serve in the Armed Forces, join a law practice, and maybe end up in politics — was suddenly and profoundly unset-tled. What I was beginning to realize is that our essential calling as Christians is to follow Jesus Christ. That's it! That calling comes to us through the waters of baptism, the sign and seal of God's grace. Every other calling in life is just an extension of that basic calling. We are called to follow Jesus in everything we do, including our vocation (which is just another word for calling) or profession (another distinctively Christian word). And it was this essential calling, which I could not clearly articulate then, that was exerting its influence in my life and was turning my vocational plans upside down. I'm not saying we all need to be ministers: for someone else, it might have meant that they would have followed the vocational path into law and politics, and they would have served God faithfully through that vocation. But in my case, the path led to the study of theology and into ordained ministry.

That day as you and I walked toward the old house on the farm, I sensed for the first time that you also were listening for that voice of calling that would shape your vocational path. I sensed that the kid walking beside me was now a young person who, like I said before, wanted to invest his life, not just spend it.

Frederick Buechner has written probably the most frequently quoted (and sometimes misquoted) statement about vocation. He says, "The place God calls you to is the place where your deep gladness and the world's deep hunger meet." Lots of people use that line in one form or another. But few people quote the paragraph that precedes it: "The kind of work God usually calls you to is the kind of work (a) that you need most to do and (b) that the world most needs to have done. If you really get a kick out of your work, you've presumably met requirement (a), but if your work is writing TV deodorant commercials, the chances are you've missed requirement (b). On the other hand, if your work is being a doctor in a leper colony, you have probably met requirement (b), but if most of the time you're bored and depressed by it, the chances are you have not only bypassed (a) but probably aren't helping your patients much either. Neither the hair shirt nor the soft berth will do."[5]

The college freshman I mentioned at the beginning of this letter is, I think, being called into social work. His "deep gladness" seems to fit the world's "deep hunger" very nicely for that vocation. But a person could just as easily be called to computer programming, or medicine, or tree trimming, or teaching. You, of course, are struggling with what you should do with a bachelor's degree in political science and an M.B.A. in finance. But there is a larger question, and it has to do with how and where the whole range of gifts and interests that make you who you are coincides with the challenges of the world that surrounds you. Both you and the world belong to God.

By the way, I've been very impressed with the detailed analyses you've done on the investment companies with which you've interviewed — particularly your assessments of their ethics, and your critiques of how well (or how poorly) they serve their clients' interests. Clearly whatever you do, you'll be concerned about serving others. Your kindness and generosity, your energy, intelligence, and humor, and so many other gifts, were all given to you to employ in your calling. The question is: Where do your deep gladness and the world's deep hunger meet? That's where your calling waits.

Dear Jessica,

I suppose that what I was saying in my last letter to you is that faith is a matter of grace, but the more I think about it, the more I think that may sound either terribly cryptic or just theologically obscure. So let me try another tack.

God's grace, that is, God's unmerited favor (as some define it), God's unconditional acceptance of us (as others define it), God's longsuffering forgiveness and mercy (as I would probably put it) is freely given to us, and it places us under the unconditional obligation to be gracious to others. To put it a slightly different way, God's grace is the gift for which we don't ask. And receiving this gift changes everything we touch.

In that sense, God's grace is like these letters: you didn't ask for them, nor did you expect them. Like so much else in life — like life itself — they are simply given to you, and what you choose to do with them is entirely up to you. (By the way, did you know that I've been writing to you since before you were born? Tucked inside that massive baby book your mother put together to chronicle your infancy is a letter, yet unopened, that I wrote to you on the day you were born, and which I gave to you then.) How, when, and whether you receive them, they are in your hands. God's grace is like this.

I particularly like this image because grace is the motivation for my writing to you. I want you to know, to paraphrase St. Paul, the faith I have received and that I now pass along to you. The grace of God precedes us in every conceivable way, and in many ways no one can conceive. I have no doubt that this will be a recurring theme in these letters. But I want to say something else by way of beginning, something more concrete. Often when we speak of God's grace, we are in danger of lapsing into very abstract ways of talking. As with so many subjects connected to

Christian faith, our conversations about grace can threaten to become untethered and float away like balloons in a strong breeze.

For me, as a Christian, I can't really say the word *grace* without speaking a particular name. It is a name still common on the tongues of many people, so common in fact that some people call their children by this name: Jesus. The theologian to whom I am probably most indebted (and this won't surprise you) is Karl Barth. Toward the end of his life, Barth said, "The last word which I have to say as a theologian and also as a politician is not a term like 'grace,' but a name, 'Jesus Christ.'"[6]

I don't know that I would mean precisely the same thing that Barth meant in saying this, but I am compelled to say it nonetheless. Grace is not abstract or ethereal; it is rooted and grounded in the life, death, and resurrection of this singular person, Jesus of Nazareth. Let me try to explain the connection between this person and the Christian understanding of grace by taking a little theological detour, this time through the life and thought of another extraordinary person who continues to shape my thinking, Dietrich Bonhoeffer.

Bonhoeffer's life has inspired countless people; his thought continues to surprise me. And one of the most surprising of his insights has to do with how easily we can dilute the meaning of God's grace by making it an abstract quality, by disconnecting it from Jesus of Nazareth. Bonhoeffer distinguished between what he called "cheap grace" and "costly grace" in a time when many Christians in his native German homeland were selling out their faith in Jesus Christ by combining it with nationalism in the shoddy, cruel, and ultimately disgraceful alliance of church and state that gave Nazism social cache among many German Christians.

Bonhoeffer wrote to his fellow Christians in Germany and in the world at large: "Cheap grace means grace as doctrine, as principle, as system. It means forgiveness of sins as a general truth; it means God's love as merely a Christian idea of God. . . . Cheap grace means justification of sin but not of the sinner. Because grace alone does everything, everything can stay in its old ways." By contrast, costly grace, Bonhoeffer says, "is the call of Jesus Christ which causes a disciple to leave his nets and follow him. . . . It is costly, because it calls to discipleship; it is grace, because it calls us to follow Jesus Christ."[7]

Jesus of Nazareth makes sense of life for us as Christians. This person, a Palestinian Jew, is the lens through which all of life comes into focus for us. And as Jesus brings the world and life into focus for us as Christians, he also brings into focus our obligations as his followers toward others. He reframes all our loyalties and allegiances under his own lordship, reminding us that if we belong (as the Heidelberg Catechism reminds us) "body and soul, in life and in death," not to ourselves but to God, then we can't give our unconditional loyalty to our nation, our race, or our gender, nor to any ideology, leader, or, indeed, anything else under heaven that might claim our souls and our lives and divide us from God and from God's image in all humanity.

In other words, faith in Christ brings us into union with God, and therefore into union with all humanity made in God's image. Christian faith refutes every sectarian impulse we may entertain.

Christianity is not another division among humanity. Christianity is not another cult or sect that pits person against person in the name of God. I think Christianity is a *recovery* of our humanity in Jesus Christ, a way to live at peace even in the presence of our enemies. When we say the word *grace* as Christians, then, we can't own the word for ourselves while disowning others from its benefits.

It's true, of course, that many awful things have been done throughout human history in the name of Jesus Christ, but it's also true that for Christians, this name pulls us back from the brink of oblivion time and again, and grounds God's grace in time and space. This name reminds us that while God's ways ultimately are not reducible to our ways, God's ways are made known in human flesh within the limits of a particular human life. This name reminds us that God's love is more fundamental than all the base motivations of inhumanity, even when these motivations are disguised as religious, even when they are disguised as Christian. Jesus of Nazareth stands to this day as the antidote to religion that has grown self-centered, self-satisfied, self-righteous, complacent, pitiless, and proud.

So if I want to tell you anything about God's grace, I have to begin by speaking this name, *Jesus.* And if I hope to say something truly Christian, I must end in this name, too.

This is the only way a Christian can speak with confidence and integrity. This is the only way a Christian can speak in a way that recovers Christian speech from the incessant and irreverent chatter that passes for Christian piety in our time. Our model in all of this is the early church, which, at its best, found in Jesus of Nazareth a portal to the sanctity of the God of Abraham, Isaac, and Jacob, and to the wisdom of a larger world.

When I speak of God's grace, then, as a Christian, I am speaking of the God who has met us in and through Jesus of Nazareth, a real person who walked this earth, was known by other real people who walked this earth, and is still known to real people today. God's grace is not a free-floating spiritual substance.

There's no celestial grace-dispensing vending machine. Grace is the *character* of the character of God, and we know this character in Jesus of Nazareth.

To be a Christian, then, means basically just this: to follow Jesus of Nazareth. It may mean more than this, of course, but it cannot mean less than this.

So this is where I must start if I want to explain to you why I am a Christian, and what it means for us to be claimed by God's grace.

Have you read Flannery O'Connor's novel *Wise Blood?* O'Connor once described the strange "integrity" of that book's antihero, Hazel Motes, as lying in the fact that he tried "with such vigor to get rid of the ragged figure who moves from tree to tree in the back of his mind." That figure in the back of Hazel's mind, of course, was Jesus. And no fictional character was ever more Jesus-haunted than he was. Whatever integrity any of us has as Christians, as persons who try to follow Jesus, stumbling all the way, lies in the fact that we have surrendered ourselves to being Jesus-haunted. Belief in Jesus will not let us go. And we believe this is God's doing.

Many years ago I read a "theological novel" by Robert Farrar Capon, *Exit 36,* about an Episcopal priest who was trying to unravel the knotted tendrils of the life of a fellow priest that ended in suicide. At his colleague's funeral, he reflects on what it means to say that we've lost our faith, and by contrast what it means to say we have faith. Most of the time, he says, when we say we've lost our faith, "all we lost was some jury-rigged philosophy that couldn't stand up to the weather." In those moments, we sense our aloneness in this world, our vulnerability. "There is only one thing for that aloneness," he says, "and that is Jesus alone. Not faith in God, because we don't know beans about God for sure. And not faith in what Jesus means, because all you've got to filter his meaning through is an old used teabag of a mind that unclarifies everything. Not even faith in what Jesus said, because, even if he actually said it all word for word, it still gets to you only through your myopic eyes and tin ears. All that kind of 'faith,' unless you're unlucky and it doesn't fall apart on you, is about as much support as a rotten floor. The only real support is Jesus. . . . Period."[8]

And that support, of which Capon speaks, is paradoxical. When we stand at the foot of the cross, as my friend Lewie Donelson once said, even the ground drops out from under our feet. Thank God our fate does not depend on us, and neither does our faith. And, yet, it is only there, standing at the foot of the cross, with the ground crumbling beneath our feet, that we can make sense of the dangers and wonders of existence.

Your mother did a calligraphy for me once of another passage in Capon's novel. I used to have it hanging on the wall of my study when I was a pastor. It read: "The difference between the saved and the damned is simply that the saved are willing to step out and explore what God remembers, while the damned insist on hanging around inside what he forgets."[9] I believe Capon ultimately is right, because I believe that it is in Jesus of Nazareth that we glimpse God's memory and God's blessed forgetfulness.

Martin Luther, the reformer, once said something to the effect that if you want to understand God you must run to the cradle in Bethlehem where the baby Jesus lies helpless; you must rush to the foot of the cross where a man hangs broken by the powers of this world. If God really is the sort of Ultimate Being who reveals his character in the helplessness of an infant and the brokenness of an executed man, we are in a whole new ballgame of talking about God. And to be completely frank with you, I'm not sure the church has been either competent or willing to take this seriously, at least not in any sustained manner. But, according to St. Paul in 1 Corinthians 1:18–2:5, this is the mystery of the wisdom of God and the power of God that redefines everything we think of as wise and strong.

———————

Dear Jeremy,

I agree. I think a lot of people misunderstand the whole idea of "calling." They reserve the word to refer to the calling of full-time Christian service, the ordained Ministry of Word and Sacrament in our tradition. When many people think of calling, they think of pastors and priests and missionaries as called, but not other people. In reality, one of the great contributions of the Protestant Reformation was a rethinking of calling and vocation to return us to the roots of these words, to understand them again in their biblical sense as inclusive of every Christian as he or she seeks God's direction and purpose in life.

Your mother, for example, is called to teach. She once told me that she became aware of her calling as a child, and spent her youth preparing to become a teacher. She is the best teacher I've ever seen in a classroom full of first- or second-graders, and her passion and skill as a primary school teacher are what make her an enthralling professor of reading now at the university level. She tried a number of other "education-related" vocations: public school administration, research in a think-tank, even accreditation work for the state. But in the end she returned to teaching because that really is her first love, her calling. A person's calling, at its best, expresses something essential about who he or she is. Our calling taps into our deepest passions, what we most care about.

If we accept the false notion of calling as a religious matter, and fence it off from the ordinary, everyday, matters of life, we lose the beating heart of vocation, its crucial point: that God created us, that God calls us to follow Jesus, and God equips each of us to follow him in distinctive ways according to the gifts God has given us in our creation. "We are to be to others," as George MacLeod, founder of the Iona Community once said, "what Christ has become for us."[10] In other words, a Christian carpenter does not need to carve little crosses on the cabinets he builds in order to express his faith, but he does need to be to others what Christ has become for him.

You asked me recently if you could be "called" to be an investment advisor. Yes. Of course you could be! I know of several people who are called to do just that. And the questions you have raised recently about each of the investment houses with which you've interviewed lead me to believe that you are taking seriously what it would mean to be called to follow Jesus Christ in that vocation.

You've researched what ethics underlie the investment philosophy of the particular companies you've interviewed with. You've spoken with the employers with whom you've interviewed to gain a better sense of their professional ethics. You've raised concerns in our conversations about the culture of corruption that is undermining so many aspects of our society, and you've noted the relative disregard among some Christians today about these matters. You've raised important questions about the virtually "theological" assumptions many economists hold regarding the omnipotence and benevolence of the "invisible hand" behind the free market, and the rather naïve notion that these market forces inevitably purify what they touch. You've confessed that you don't have faith in the economic forces that Adam Smith and many of his contemporary followers place their faith in (that's your Calvinism at work!), and you certainly have a more robust view of the pervasiveness and tenacity of sin in the world than many economists. You have also raised the concern that perhaps certain expressions of Protestantism have become wholly owned subsidiaries of global corporate interests, a sort of "McChurch" that makes God and human beings into commodities to be marketed and sold.

In his *Credo,* which was published toward the end of his life, William Sloane Coffin observed that "Jesus saw the demonic side when he saw money as a rival god capable of inspiring great devotion. . . . No wonder Jesus talked more about money than any other subject except the kingdom of God."[11] As a student of finance and as a person reflecting on your calling, you are particularly well-situated to reflect theologically on money, and to call into question the strange devotions that develop around its possession and uses, and the silence (you could almost say the sacred taboos) that our society and church accord finances.

And I am glad to see you're raising these issues. Preachers can try, but by and large they lack the credibility of businesspeople, of people trained as you are in finance and economics, of people invested in corporate leadership. Perhaps the only revolution of faith we can expect to touch the economic disparities in our culture must be led by businesspeople who hear again the prophetic message of the Bible of public justice that has been neglected and ignored in recent years in favor of private forms of spirituality focused on individualized "inner peace" and "personal morality." Perhaps only a savvy Christian business leader can credibly raise concerns about the injustice of a society in which the top 1% of the population owns over 40% of the wealth.

When I was a student in Aberdeen, the chaplain of the British House of Commons spoke to us one day. He chose as his subject a book written the year I was born, the book written by George MacLeod that I quoted to you earlier in this letter. He said that this book, read when he was a young man, shaped his entire ministry, indeed, his entire life. The passage that most deeply affected him was this one:

> I simply argue that the Cross be raised again at the center of the marketplace as well as on the steeple of the church. I am recovering the claim that Jesus was not crucified in a cathedral between two candles, but on a cross between two thieves; on the town garbage-heap; at a crossroad so cosmopolitan that they had to write his title in Hebrew and in Latin and in Greek (or shall we say in English, in Bantu, and in Afrikaans?); at the kind of place where cynics talk smut, and thieves curse, and soldiers gamble. Because that is where He died. And that is what He died about. And that is where churchmen should be and what churchmanship should be about.[12]

MacLeod saw it as every Christian's vocation to follow Jesus of Nazareth in the marketplaces of the world, and he rejected the idea that discipleship is just a religious matter, something we do in a church building but that does not affect our everyday lives. MacLeod, and the young people who followed him out to Iona, off the west coast of Scotland, rebuilt the ancient monastic ruins of that sacred island to house a living community where people of Christian and other faiths could come together to pray and work and prepare themselves to serve others around the world.

His comments remind me of a distinctively American theologian's reflections on the same topic, Clarence Jordan's. Jordan was the founder of the Koinonia Farm experiment in Georgia and an inspiration for the Habitat for Humanity movement. In one of his most memorable sermons, Jordan said, "Faith is not belief in spite of evidence but a life in scorn of the consequences." Jordan's translation of Hebrews 11:1 says it even better: "Faith is the activation of our aspirations, the life based on unseen realities. It is conviction translated into deeds. In short, it is the word become flesh."[13]

Who was it who said, "Love God and damn the consequences"? I can't remember. But that's the idea. We are called to follow the way of Jesus of Nazareth, to practice his life of self-giving love in the midst of this world we inhabit and in the pursuit of our various vocations, remembering that God created this world in love, and loves this world (all of this world!) still.

⎯⎯⎯⎯⎯

Dear Jessica,

This morning I was rereading a book I've loved almost to death. The paperback spine is broken. The glue holding it together is dried and crumbling. Its pages are falling out because I've reread it so many times over the years. It was written by someone whose life and ideas deeply influenced me as a young person, Carlyle Marney. His name is nearly forgotten these days, but he was a person of extraordinary originality, a brilliant maverick, with a voice like God's, only deeper. Reading his words made me think of you: "I have for years been running into men who are better than their creeds. Creeds kept long make little men. Men who are bigger than their creeds are living a Credo, an 'I believe,' an 'I am committed,' but the content of commitment is not yet too rigidly spelled out. Credo has to be very careful what it says it believes, and over some words so sacred their meaning is always in doubt, Credo stammers. At no single spot does Credo claim that the Mystery is pristinely clear lest it close off new perspectives. Yet, here and there, 'I believe' can focus."[14]

I appreciate the way Marney differentiates between creeds and credo. The word *credo* is Latin for "I believe." Reading this passage, I thought about you because your credo, your personal "I believe," is so much bigger than any single creed. I think that's at least partially why sometimes you have a hard time identifying yourself as a Christian. But this struggle of the soul to understand your faith rather than to accept without critical reflection the creeds given to you by others is an essentially faithful undertaking. It reminds me of the engagement between Jesus and his disciples when he asks them, "Who do people say that I am?" The disciples told him that some people thought Jesus was John the Baptist returned from the dead, or Elijah or another of the ancient prophets. And Jesus pressed the disciples, "But who do you say that I am?" (Mark 8:27-29). "What," Jesus seems to ask them, "is your credo?"

Some people today think Jesus of Nazareth was a half-mad Galilean prophet, a good man, a wise teacher, a faith healer. Some people think he was a zealot whose revolutionary ideas frightened the Sadducees into plotting his execution at the hands of Rome. Some people think he was a gifted rabbi who universalized the Judaism of his day into a faith for all humanity. Some people think he is a violent apocalyptic figure, broken on the wheel of human history, only to be avenged in a coming age. Others believe he is the archetypal peacemaker who laid down his life to show us God's way of peace over the power of the sword. Each of these perspectives, and many, many more besides, can be scrupulously documented by the work of scholars around the world. But Jesus does not ask us for a term-paper religion, in which we give him what everyone else says about him, complete with footnotes and appendices. Jesus wants credo from us. And credo, the "I believe" kind of faith, the quality of faith that God and life evoke from us, is not satisfied by our saying, "Well, *some* people believe this and *others* believe that." It requires of us to simply and honestly stand before this Jesus who comes to us as Albert Schweitzer once said, "as One unknown, without a name, as of old, by the lake-side," and to respond to his question, "Who do *you* say that I am?"[15]

That kind of faith may stutter and stammer, as Marney said. That kind of faith may stumble like the disciples did, unable or unwilling to follow even after they realized who Jesus was. A *credo* may lack the eloquence of the poet and the subtlety of a systematic theologian, but it is your very own statement, the thing you must say with your whole life when confronted with the astonishing mystery of God's Being and the astonishing mystery of your own existence.

Anyway, when I read that passage from Marney's book today I remembered the job interview you told me about, the one with the woman who told you that her organization is "a Christian organization." You told me that she asked you whether you'd have a problem working with Christians, and at first I just laughed. But then she described in detail the specific "Christian" beliefs the organization held, and they weren't so much matters of faith as they were positions on political issues. And when she finished, you were hesitant even to say that you are a Christian because you did not want to identify yourself with beliefs she and her organization espoused. You said, "I think I am open enough to work with almost anyone," but you suspected they would not want to hire you if they really knew you.

Well, knowing you as I do, it's their loss!

What I said to you then, if you remember, was simply a statement of fact. "Remember, Jessica, you are baptized."

No matter what anyone says, no matter how narrowly or how broadly they construe the Christian faith or membership in the church, you are baptized. No matter what you believe or don't believe at any particular moment of your life, you cannot change the fact that you are baptized. Baptism is the sign and seal of God's grace toward us, God's grace expressed to us before we are able to make any claim on God. This sign of water made on your forehead long ago, this cross traced on your skin in the name of the Trinity, is indelible.

During all the years I served as a pastor, on every occasion I stood at the baptismal font with a baby in my arms, at the close of the child's baptism I would say to that infant, who could not understand me, and to all the children in our church, young and old, "You belong to God. We entrust you to God's care, that you may rest in the hollow of God's hand. Be sure of this and never doubt: what God holds in his hand, no one can snatch away from him."

I say this because I have become rather disgusted by Christians who treat belonging to Christ like some kind of exclusive club membership.

A few days ago, a rather well-known Christian personality died — I won't name names here, but if you follow the news at all, you probably know. He was famous, some might say notorious, for his pronouncements about what God does and does not approve of, about whom God loves and whom God hates. He was a bastion of religious certitude and, frankly, at times, of narrow-minded bigotry in the name of Christ. The day he died, the press called the office of one of my colleagues and asked for a quote. My colleague, Ted Wardlaw, declined the interview, but later told me what he wanted to say (and, indeed, what he did say in a subsequent sermon): "I believe that today this man was ushered into the gates of heaven and into the presence of a God who is vastly bigger and more grace-filled than he ever imagined."

I am glad God's grace is a lot bigger than what passes as "grace" administered by God's fan clubs. I am embarrassed by the smallness of so many religiously-minded people, and I become angry when their small-mindedness wounds a person like you, because you are bigger than their creed.

This is not just a matter of tolerance, as you've heard me say a million times. Tolerance is just the bare minimal expectation of a civil society. Tolerance expresses a kind of forbearance, and can be just another form of one-upmanship: "I believe this, and you believe that, and though I'm right and you're wrong, I'll tolerate you!" That is all tolerance maintains, and it represents a minimal response to difference.

People of faith can rise above this minimal level, if we want to. After all, there's not a faith in the world that does not recognize that God is very, very big, unimaginably big, so big we can't even comprehend God's God-ness. God is Mystery, hidden, beyond all human knowledge and wisdom. Jews believe this. Muslims too. Hindus, Buddhists, all sorts and conditions of faiths believe this, in some version or another. Christians definitely believe this. Blaise Pascal, on one of those scattered scraps of paper that were gathered up into his *Pensées,* said: "God being thus hidden, any religion that does not say that God is hidden is not true, and any religion which does not explain why does not instruct. Ours does all thus. Verily thou art a God that hidest thyself."[16] And, yet, there's something about the contemporary religious climate in our country (maybe everywhere these days) that seems to demand that we make definitive statements on behalf of God to demonstrate how faithful we are.

I'm astonished when I hear Christians claim to know God's position on everything from phonics in reading instruction to housing policies for urban Chicago. God may indeed have a housing policy in the works for urban Chicago, but I don't have a lot of clarity on what it is, and I wouldn't want it to be a condition for membership in the church at any rate.

There's something about reverence for God that demands that we shut up sometimes. And how can we say "I love God," whom we have never seen, if we cannot find it in us to love the only images of God that bear God's copyright? That was the question asked by the author of 1 John.

So maybe we are supposed to tolerate others. Maybe that's the least we can do. And maybe we are supposed to respect them too, since they and we share a common humanity. But maybe we are also supposed to reverence others; if, that is, they are created in the image of the invisible God.

Anyway, I was thinking of you today when I read the passage from Marney about people who are bigger than their creed. It occurs to me that not only are some people bigger than their creeds. God is too. Thank God.

Dear Jeremy,

Thank you for reading James Chatham's book *Is It I, Lord?* for me, and for giving me your feedback on it. Like I said, I wanted to get an unbiased reading from a young adult as to whether it would make a good text for my Call to Ministry class in the fall. Chatham, of course, focuses specifically on the call to pastoral ministry, and that's not necessarily what you've been wrestling with in your own life, but I felt sure your reading of it would give me a better sense of whether the book would work with our students. I will plan to include the book in my required reading list for the course next fall.

I'm pleased with your decision to take the position in fundraising. I know the little organization that has offered you the position. It is struggling, but it has a great mission, and it really needs the help of someone who understands finances. You'll enjoy helping them build relationships with pastors and churches, and your experience in development and institutional advancement will be welcome.

I know this isn't the sort of position you expected to take with an M.B.A. You've mentioned several times your frustration at watching classmates from college and graduate school, especially some of your fraternity brothers, who are already making lots of money while your professional life seems to have stalled. At least it seems that way to you.

The last thing you want is for your dad to tell you that money isn't everything. You already know that's true. You've seen what money can do, for good and bad. You don't need a lecture on that subject, and you surely don't need me getting all nostalgic with my misty memories of when your mother and I started out in married life thirty years ago, too poor to sustain a checking account, and how much fun we had in a two-room apartment eating beans and cornbread until it ran out our ears, both of us working at department stores in the same shopping center while I was in seminary. But we were as poor as church mice, and it really was fun . . . Okay. Enough already.

What I should respond to, because it represents such a profound understanding of your own emerging sense of vocation, is your reflection on the public role Christian faith has neglected, and the responsibility we have to re-engage society as a whole. I'm pleased that you're enjoying the copy of Dietrich Bonhoeffer's *Life Together* I gave you for Christmas. I agree, it should be required reading for every seminarian. In fact, if I had my way, Bonhoeffer's *Cost of Discipleship* would be required reading for all Christians. Since you're enjoying *Life Together* so much, I'll also get a copy of his *Letters and Papers from Prison* for you.

What you are saying about learning to follow Jesus in your vocation is similar to what Bonhoeffer says about faith: "Faith is participation in this being of Jesus (incarnation, cross, and resurrection). Our relation to God is not a 'religious' relationship to the highest, most powerful, and best Being imaginable — that is not authentic transcendence — but our relation to God is a new life in 'existence for others,' through participation in the being of Jesus. The transcendental is not infinite and unattainable tasks, but the neighbor who is within reach in any given situation."[17]

What I think Bonhoeffer is saying is that we don't participate in God, in other words, by grasping for higher, greater "divine" power, or by aspiring to distant metaphysical abstractions. In some ways, Bonhoeffer is just being a good Lutheran in saying this. Martin Luther, almost five hundred years ago, countered what he called a "theology of glory," which tries to define God by climbing the ladder of lofty theological abstractions, with a "theology of the cross," that demands that we limit our statements about God, God's nature, and God's character to what can be said in light of God's revelation of himself in Jesus of Nazareth. Luther focuses on St. Paul's admonition to know Christ and him crucified; thus his theological approach was called a "theology of the cross." Bonhoeffer's insight is simply an extension of Luther's "theology of the cross."

Real transcendence is not about finding God in some inner experience, or via a scholastic undertaking, or some otherworldly endeavor. If it is true, as one sociologist of religion has said, that people in contemporary North America are yearning for a "transcendent experience of the sacred," a transformative engagement with "the self-transcending and life-changing core of all true religion,"[18] then, Bonhoeffer would assure us, they need look no further than the face of the humanity at their doorstep if they wish to see God. The holy is *always* within our reach, if we will only reach out to our neighbor. I think you'll find that to be true in your new neighborhood, among people desperately in need of basic services such as dental care and a bag of groceries.

Seminaries today are bursting at the seams with people who have sought all kinds of experiences of transformation and who have tried to fill the void in their lives with all sorts of things. When I meet them in a classroom, they are often at a point of supreme readiness to hear something real, something other than the old advertising claims recycled into messages of Christianity. I cannot tell you how often one of these folks — a former lobbyist, an attorney, a business executive, a surgeon, a banker, the list could go on and on — will come across some passage in Bonhoeffer: a question — "What do we really believe? I mean, believe in such a way that we stake our lives on it?" — or a challenge — "The church is the church only when it exists for others" — or a message of personal rededication — "I must tell [people] of every calling what it means to live in Christ, to exist for others."[19] And reading these passages, their eyes light up, and they see amid the ordinary moments of life a calling worth pursuing. Bonhoeffer speaks of disciples as persons who, after being called, can never return to their nets again — referring, of course, to the fact that some of the first disciples of Jesus were fishermen who gave up their fishing to follow him. I sense among many of these men and women in seminary today that they have sought the "answer" in so many endeavors, in achievements, in professional success, in wealth, in personal indulgence (often of the most "spiritual" kinds), and that reading Bonhoeffer they "come to themselves," and realize that no matter what they do in the future, they can never return to their "nets" again.

Reading Bonhoeffer myself, especially in light of some of the criticisms you and I have shared regarding the contemporary church, I wonder what "nets" the church might yet need to escape. Toward the close of his life, only a few months before the Nazis hanged him, Bonhoeffer said, "In particular, our own church will have to take the field against the vices of hubris, power-worship, envy, and humbug, as the roots of all evil. It will have to speak of moderation, purity, trust, loyalty, constancy, patience, discipline, humility, contentment, and modesty."[20]

The only time I remember noticing the word *humbug* before in literature was in Dickens, and it was connected to the exclamation, *Bah!* But I think I agree wholeheartedly with Bonhoeffer. There are days when we read Bonhoeffer together in class and his words sound like shouts in a river canyon or trumpet blasts in a cathedral, so loudly do the echoes from his letters written half a century ago in a Nazi jail thunder off the walls of our contemporary experience. I think you'll hear the echoes too, the urgency of the message for a church too wrapped up in its own self-interests, self-promotion, and self-righteousness to attend to others, a society in which power has distorted every human sentiment into cynicism and in which lying in the service of partisanship has become nothing more than "spin." We'll talk more this weekend.

I'm proud of you, and of your work, and of your emerging vocation — though neither of us knows exactly what that vocation will entail or where it will lead.

Dear Jessica,

Lately I've taken to referring to myself (only half-jokingly) as a Zen Calvinist. What I mean by this is that I am pretty much at peace with life or, to use a rather archaic phrase from another era, I've made my peace with God, which, as a Calvinist, comes to the same thing. I have always appreciated the modesty of John Calvin (on this I'm not joking at all!). Calvin humbly recognized the fact that "our mind is incapable of entertaining God's essence." He believed that if we are to understand what God is like we must regard "the world itself as a kind of mirror" in which to catch fleeting glimpses of God, "in so far as it concerns us to know God."[21] That last little phrase is especially nice, "in so far as it concerns us to know God," because it assumes that there are things about God (undoubtedly many, many things) that just are not any of our business.

As a Christian — as a follower of Jesus of Nazareth — I am especially struck by the way in which Jesus struggled with his consciousness of God, and how Jesus came to terms with his mission in the world. Every one of us must discern in the world the road on which God has set us, the mission (if you will) to which God calls us. Amid the ambiguities and paradoxes of life, amid life's contradictions and the sometimes agonizing choices between competing goods and lesser evils, we live our days trusting in the God who loves freedom more than safety, whose creation is an act of unending self-giving, and whose love is more powerful than anything in the world, including our sin.

All three parts of this credo of mine were hard-won. It took me an especially long time to make peace with God and God's world in the matter of freedom and safety. I wanted a world with guardrails on it, a world with training wheels you never outgrow. God, apparently, does not want such a world. To explain what I mean, I need to tell you a story about someone you never knew.

Keith, my younger brother, died the year you were born. He was only twelve years old. I was in my late twenties. Born with a congenital heart defect, every day of his life was a gift fraught with terrors, often painful, often dreadful and dreary, sometimes glorious, and never taken for granted. I do not know how my parents endured those years, the constant possibility of his death hanging over them, rushing to the hospital at all hours, the endless procession of emergency procedures, needles inserted, blood drawn, the pain he knew as a matter of course, simply the cost of his survival; the suffering my parents felt, utterly helpless to stop his pain or to alter the inevitable.

The philosophical problem of God's goodness and human suffering was, for me, a family affair. The struggle over this "problem" came to a head one summer Sunday, shortly after noon. I had preached that morning on "The Shaking of the Foundations." The sermon text was Isaiah 6. Like many sermons I preached in those early years of ministry, this one hovered about six feet off of the ground, failing to connect or relate clearly or apply directly to the lives of the people I served. I operated pretty safely in my head. The sermon's application happened thirty minutes after I left the pulpit, when I walked into our house, and your mother, then pregnant with you, met me at the door with the words, "Your mother just called. Keith died a few minutes ago." I fell into her arms and wept. My foundations shook.

I continued to weep for months thereafter as the aftershocks continued. I wept through an outpouring of words, especially through sermons, when there were no tears left for my eyes to shed. I preached the same question a dozen different ways: *How could we claim that God is good if God created such a world as this, a world in which innocent children suffer all their lives and die young?* I remember saying to someone that even a fool like me could have thought up a better world than this.

Grief is the most powerful constellation of emotions in the human universe, and grief drove me for months after Keith's death. Most of what I believe about God and the world was forged, to some extent, either in relation to the grief we anticipated while living with Keith for twelve years, or in relation to the grief we felt after he died, or in relation to the grief I continued to fear every time I looked into your mother's, or your, or Jeremy's eyes, and the eyes of everyone I loved.

Grief is the price tag that life places on love. Some day the bill comes due for us all, and this is one tab that nobody else can pick up for you.

What I learned cannot be squeezed on a bumper sticker, and no one can learn the most important things in life for any one else, so I know there's no sense in my regurgitating my experiences wholesale in the hope that I can save you time, effort, and tears, and there's no way I can abstract the "lessons" or "morals" from all of this anyway. What I can say is this: Keith has been dead for almost twenty-five years now, and, along the way, I've made peace with God's world as well as with God for creating this world.

The problem, of course, is freedom, the freedom of God's creation. It's not a philosopher's gambit, like the question whether this is the best of all possible worlds, that keeps me up at night, at least not anymore. Over the years I simply have come to see that the phenomenal beauty and wonder of creation requires freedom, dangerous freedom, crazy, random, chaotic freedom. The safety and security I wanted so badly would make for a monochromatic and mediocre world. Only a world in which it's possible for twelve-year-old brothers to die can offer the joy that lit up that same brother's face when we visited the ancient Caddo Mounds in our native East Texas together a few months before he died, and stood atop these artifacts of antiquity marveling at the beauty of our native landscape, surveying the vast alluvial plain bordered with hickory, pine, and chestnut, neither of us knowing how little time we had left to breathe the same air in the precious and fragile thing we call life.

I have joked that I never understood the vulnerability of the Creator in making that which is free and dangerous until you got your driver's license. The day I took you to the Texas Department of Public Safety (the irony of the nomenclature seemed complete that day) to get your license, it occurred to me that I had played a key role in bringing into the world a force of incalculable potential for pain as well as for good, because once you had that license a whole world of people would be placed in mortal peril. But, all joking aside, I had already learned this lesson about vulnerability. I learned it as I stood beside my brother's casket and said goodbye to him. As angry as I was then at God and as much as I grieved and empathized with my parents' grief, I believe that none of us grieved as deeply for Keith as God did.

The Nobel laureate Elie Wiesel says that his teacher, Rabbi Saul Lieberman, once told him: "One can — and must — love God. One can challenge him and even be angry with him, but one must also pity him. 'Do you know which of all the characters in the Bible is most tragic?' he asked me. 'It is God, blessed be his name, God whose creatures so often disappoint and betray him.'"[22]

A machine does not have the power to betray; a robot might be programmed always to function predictably; but creations act. Freedom is necessary to creation. And the first victim of creation's freedom, abused and shattered, is always God.

For me as a Christian, then, the cross of Jesus of Nazareth makes sense of creation's freedom, good and bad. "Jesus," as one of our Presbyterian confessions says, "a Palestinian Jew, lived among his own people and shared their needs, temptations, joys, and sorrows. He expressed the love of God in word and deed and became a brother to all kinds of sinful men."[23] But his life of love led Jesus directly into conflict with the ideals, the religion, and

51

the national aspirations of humanity which rejected him and condemned him to death. Jesus lived the sort of life that provokes crosses in this sort of world. The cross of Jesus brings into focus the terrible consequences of the world's freedom, and highlights the freedom of God to suffer for those who reject him.

This is why Joseph Sittler said, "Unless the God before whom we sit, and at whom we gaze, and about whom we think — unless that God has the tormented shape of our human existence, he isn't God enough. We ask, 'Why did God become human?' And the answer is that the God who wants to be the source of our order must become the horror of our disorder, or he has no authority."[24]

If God can love this creation, with all that creation has cost him, then I suppose we can love creation too. Of course, saying it this way makes life sound like a set of transactions. And it is not. God loves creation because God is love, and creation is that which God created in love to be loved. For all its terrors, horrors and cesspits, creation still takes our breath away.

All of which brings me to the Zen part of my Zen Calvinism, or maybe, more precisely, it's the Tao part. One of my favorite chapters of the *Tao Te Ching* asks

> Do you think you can take over the universe and improve it? I do not believe it can be done.
>
> The universe is sacred.
> You cannot improve it.
> If you try to change it, you will ruin it.
> If you try to hold it, you will lose it.[25]

It was pure sophomoric arrogance that led me to believe I could imagine a better world than the one God created. Fallen as I believe the world is (yes, I really am a Calvinist!) it is freely fallen and freely redeemed. The ancient Christian thinker Irenaeus may even have been right when he said that when humanity fell we may have fallen forward. Our sins are real sins committed in freedom and in bondage and in every state in between; and our sins are really forgiven, not just excused or winked at by the God who is fully free to act as God is pleased to act. And we can rest cradled in the hands of a living God who suffers at our hands the consequences of his own passion for freedom, trusting, just trusting ourselves and everyone we love to a mercy and wisdom that in its silence is more eloquent than any human words.

A few nights ago, your mother and I sat in the backyard as the summer afternoon heat gave way to a soft evening breeze. The silence was unbroken but by the rustling of the limbs of elms and oaks, the darkness unmediated except by lightning bugs, and the stillness challenged only by a Mexican freetail bat that darted through our backyard feasting on mosquitoes. As in the gathering darkness we sat, I wondered at the uncomfortable, but perfect, mixture of things created in that tiny space under a canopy of infinite space. We are so small, so infinitesimally small, to wonder at matters so large. I began to smile, then to laugh out loud. Other than silence, what response but laughter is appropriate to an awareness of our true proportion in this universe? I wish I had a portrait of John Calvin laughing with the abandon of the laughing Buddha. You know the fat Buddha statues, don't you? The ones that show the "Enlightened One" roaring, his great belly quaking, his head thrown back with the laughter of an infant? I'd love to have a laughing Calvin, at peace with God's world because God is at peace with us.

George MacDonald wrote in his *Diary of an Old Soul*, "Some times, hard-trying, it seems I cannot pray for doubts and pain and anger and all strife. . . . All things seem rushing straight into the dark. But the dark still is God." If God is the Being, Holy Being, Being of beings, in whom we (together with the whole universe) live and move, and nothing, not even the darkest nights of the soul, are foreign to God because God has traversed every road we travel, then it hardly matters in the end if we are walking through darkness or light. We are living, moving, and being in God. It gives me hope to think that Paul Faber was right when he said: "I think when the sun rises upon them, some people will be surprised to find how far they have got in the dark."[26]

I pray this is true, because so much of the time, the life of faith feels to me like fumbling in a dark room for the light switch, or maybe sitting in the dark watching the stars and realizing I know so little and must trust God for so much.

Dear Jeremy,

You're right. One of the difficulties with responding to a particular calling is the awareness that choosing to go down one path means choosing not to go down another. That is part of what Robert Frost was getting at when he wrote about the road not taken. Frost was thinking of his own vocation as a poet, realizing that his calling would require enormous discipline, and that if he wished to travel the poet's road, there were other paths he would never be able to walk.

To some degree, these choices are inevitable in life. To put it theologically, we are finite creatures: we can't do everything.

When I started college, I was spending as much time pursuing my love of music as some of my friends who were music majors. But given the amount of practice it takes to perform well as a musician and the work it takes to do well at biblical studies and theology, I realized before too long that I could either be a pretty good theologian or a pretty fair musician, but not both. I simply did not have the talent to do both well. I chose to pursue theology. Sometimes I miss the joy of performing in a jazz ensemble or a rhythm-and-blues band, though I still love playing the piano or guitar (by myself and well out of earshot from others), and music remains a vital part of my life. But I had to focus intently on the study of theology if I hoped to do well in pursuit of my calling, and I couldn't have done that if I kept up the level of practice in music that I was doing in college. I had to make a choice.

You are a person with many gifts, and those gifts could take you in any number of different directions, and it may be that your primary vocation (whatever that turns out to be) will allow you to engage several of your gifts. I have also found this to be true. As much as I loved music, I have also loved writing, and my interest in writing has integrated nicely into my vocation as a pastor and teacher. I have friends who have integrated their music and their theological callings in some creative ways, though they clearly had more talent in these areas than I did. One of the things I loved most about being a pastor was the range of gifts and interests that are called for in what someone has called "the general practice of ministry." But we all have limits, and part of being human is knowing them and embracing those limits.

You mentioned that several of your friends have resisted taking any particular vocational road because they don't want to exclude any of their interests. While it may be possible to pursue several interests and use many gifts, my hunch is that inevitably when we choose in favor of one or another vocation we will sacrifice something else. It really is as simple as saying that we cannot simultaneously take every road on every trip. And I have seldom come to a crossroads at which I didn't regret my limitations. I resonate with Frost's longing as he stands at the divergence of paths, wishing he could walk down both at the same time:

> And sorry I could not travel both
> And be one traveler, long I stood
> And looked down one as far as I could
> To where it bent in the undergrowth;
>
> Then took the other, as just as fair,
> And having perhaps the better claim.[27]

The reason Frost tells his story with a sigh is because of the regret he feels at the good choice he made. It's the same regret we all feel when we reflect on the choices we have made and the losses these choices have entailed. This is the genius of Frost's poetic insight. Even wonderful choices entail losses.

When your mother and I decided to leave the United States so I could do my Ph.D. in theology at the University of Aberdeen we had to sell almost everything we owned and put the remainder in storage. We left our family and a close-knit circle of friends at the church in Itasca. We moved to a country we had never before visited, where we did not know anyone. We experienced genuine loss, and real regrets. The young women who were your mother's closest friends gave us as a going-away gift a quilt they had made. The pattern was titled "Crosses and Losses." When the time came to leave Scotland, we had made so many good friends there and had come to love our life there so much, it was just as hard to return to the United States as it had been to leave in the first place. Maybe this is the way it should be. Maybe our choices between the roads we take should never come easy.

I believe that the vocational choices you face are made all the more difficult because there are several areas in which you can imagine investing your life, and it is never easy to determine (at least in the privacy of your own heart) precisely where your passions are best invested in God's world.

John Calvin, as a young man, longed to lead a life of quiet scholarship. That was, in fact, what he was seeking when he passed through the city of Geneva, Switzerland, in 1536. A Renaissance humanist, already a published scholar, a lover of literature and law, Calvin knew his own passions well, and he chose a vocation, private scholarship, that seemed to correspond to them. But William Farel, a church leader in Geneva, recognized in Calvin, along with his scholarship, other capacities that could aid the reformation. Calvin himself tells the story better than I can:

> And after learning that my heart was set upon devoting myself to private studies, for which I wished to keep myself free from other pursuits, and finding that he gained nothing by entreaties, he [Farel] proceeded to utter the imprecation that God would curse my retirement and the tranquility of the studies which I sought, if I should withdraw and refuse to help, when the necessity was so urgent. By this imprecation I was so terror-struck, that I gave up the journey I had undertaken; but sensible of my natural shyness and timidity, I would not tie myself to any particular office.[28]

Calvin, in the end, had to overcome even his natural shyness for the sake of his calling. As the leader of the church in Geneva, he had the opportunity to employ his many gifts as a scholar, but his life was far from quiet as he preached, taught, and led. I'm sure there were many days when Calvin longed for the peace and quiet of a scholarly retreat far from the conflicts of Geneva. And I suspect that when he thought of all he had lost by responding to Farel's entreaties (and God's call!), he felt some regret from time to time. But Calvin's calling, thrust upon him by others, was sure, and it sustained him throughout a turbulent life. You may not get a William Farel (few of us do), but you will have others who will help you sort out your calling. In the end, the choices will be yours, and so will the consequences.

Having said this, I would add that many, if not most, of your gifts will be useful in whatever vocation you choose, and in your various avocations. God gives us gifts to be used, and seldom do we need to abandon altogether some interest or ability entirely in order to pursue a particular vocation.

Remember also that vocations and careers are not necessarily identical. William Stringfellow was an attorney by training, but he was also one of the most erudite and prophetic Christian writers of the late twentieth century. Stringfellow once observed,

> Biblically, vocation does not have any connotation limited to work. Vocation pertains to the whole of life, including work, of course, if and when there is work, but embracing every other use of time, every other engagement of body and mind, every other circumstance in life. . . . Moreover, in the gospel, vocation always bears an implication of immediacy — there is really no such thing as preparing to under-

take one's vocation when one grows up or when one gradu-
ates or when one obtains a certain position or when one
gets to a certain place. Vocation is always here and now,
without anxiety where one might be tomorrow. . . . Vocation has to do with recognizing life as a gift and honoring
the gift in living. . . . In the gospel, vocation means being a
human being, now, and being neither more nor less than a
human being now.[29]

His comments remind me of something a colleague once said,
that St. Augustine had gotten the church off track because he
was so preoccupied with personal salvation. Before Augustine,
he said, the primary focus of the Christian message was vocation: Christ's calling us to follow him. I'm not sure my colleague's history of doctrine is entirely accurate, but his theology
of vocation is on target. Fundamentally, the gospel is about our
being called to follow Jesus.

Two contrasting but complementary pictures of what G. K.
Chesterton famously called "the Christian thing" — that is, the
goal and purpose of the Christian faith — are represented by vocation and salvation. We are, in a sense, "saved" through God's
"calling" of us, in that the ways in which we follow Christ in this
world not only serve others, but work for our redemption.

This is why another colleague of mine was so right when he
observed wryly that there are some people God can only save by
making preachers of them. I think this was certainly true for me.
But it may also be true that there are some people God can only
save by making physicians of them, or teachers, or craftsmen, or
parents. "What we do for a living" is never completely irrelevant
to God's calling us to follow Jesus Christ — not if what we do for
a living has any real connection to our lives.

59

Dear Jessica,

This morning as I walked into my office, I saw that letter you wrote to me when you were very small. Do you remember it? You wrote it on a Post-it note and left it on the desk in my study between worship services. This was when we lived in Brenham. Your letter reads:

> Dear Pastor,
> I believe God
> Can do anythin-
> g. So can
> my daddy.
> Jessica

I put that letter in a frame, and it sits on a bookshelf right in front of my set of Karl Barth's *Church Dogmatics*. The first sentence of your letter relates directly to the subject of my last letter to you.

In almost every survey I've come across, whenever church people are asked what their biggest theological question is, they respond with some version of "Why do bad things happen to good people?" to use Rabbi Harold Kushner's phrase, or "How can a good God allow evil to happen?"[30] What's always striking to me is that the question, however you want to formulate it, is necessary only because we believe that God is good. If we believed that God were bad or morally indifferent, then the problem of evil and suffering would not be a theological problem at all.

Of course there are other theological problems that trouble us. I can't help thinking of the rather silly questions theologians and philosophers have sometimes asked, like, "Could God, in his infinite power, create a rock so heavy that he cannot lift it?" That one isn't all that different from the old "How many angels can dance on the head of a pin?" (Actually, the more I read about quantum physics, the less silly that question sounds to me, but we'll leave that to one side for now!)

But the problem of evil and suffering is a "problem" and it presents us with an irreducible "question" because we Christians believe that God's almightiness and God's love are both essential to who God is. Neither God's goodness nor God's power is up for grabs. If we give up on God's love, and imagine that there is no God (or heaven, or hell below us, as John Lennon asks us to try), or that God is not good (as C. S. Lewis feared at times after his wife's death, as he tells us in his book *A Grief Observed*), then the "problem," insofar as it is a theological problem, is solved, and the "question" is laid to rest. [31]

On the other hand, if we give up on God's power, and view God simply as impotent, incompetent, a bumbling under-achiever (in the tradition of some of Woody Allen's jokes), then the "problem" also vanishes in a puff of smoke. Abracadabra!

But if we want to hold together these two faith statements, then we've got a problem that will not go away — at least not in the face of the evidence of human history. This is a problem we have confronted for as long as people have looked up to heaven, from Job to the Psalms of lament to Jesus, and cried out, "My God, my God, why have you forsaken me?"

You and I have talked about this before, I know, and it remains a serious obstacle for the faith of many thoughtful and good people. My best friend in high school — he was the very person who brought me to church as a teenager — finally gave up on Christianity when he was a young adult, becoming an atheist because he could not reconcile the God of our Sunday school lessons and the experiences of human suffering he became aware of as an adult.

This is another of those places in our faith where bumper-sticker slogans fall far short — but frankly so do many of the most carefully reasoned arguments of world-class theologians and philosophers, too.

My own faith has crashed against these rocks periodically, and has sought safe harbors more or less successfully from time to time. My reflections on the problem of God's goodness and God's power, and the persistence of evil and suffering, have been intellectual as well as spiritual, because both the mind and the heart are involved in theology.

I have come to believe that as followers of Jesus of Nazareth our understanding of power has to be at odds with the way most people see power in our world. Jesus lived exactly the life God called him to live. Jesus taught. Jesus lived in obedience to God. Jesus healed the sick, ate with and forgave sinners, and gave his life away for the sake of others (including those who treated him with disrespect and cruelty). He refused to return evil for evil, but blessed those who cursed him and extended mercy to those who killed him. And God placed God's stamp of approval on his life, the whole of his life, in all its vulnerability and utter selflessness, by raising him from the dead. We say that God is almighty, but we never really understand the character of God's might until God renders up his own life for us in Jesus of Nazareth. The character of God's almightiness is pure, self-giving love.

This doesn't make the "problem" of God's goodness and God's power in a world of pain and suffering go away. If anything, it accentuates the difficulties in the problem, and makes it God's problem too. But it also provides a framework in which to understand the nature of the problem. It provides a way for us to live our lives as faithfully as we know how. Jesus said that if we want to be perfect (meaning complete and whole) as God is perfect, then we must be merciful. "At a time when the world seems to be spinning hopelessly out of control," as our beloved Willie Nelson sings, I find great comfort in this fact: that God does not expect me to render judgment, just to act mercifully, if I want to reflect God's character. If Christian faith can make us merciful, then there's truth in it, don't you think? And, maybe, there's hope, too, that power can be redeemed.

Dear Jeremy,

It was great talking with you today. You have indeed wrestled with your vocation, your calling, for several months, as you said. But I have to tell you that your decision isn't really as much of a surprise for those who know you as it is for you.

After we got off the phone, I went back to the guest room here at the college where mother and I are staying, and I told her what we talked about. I told her simply what you had said, that as you were praying in worship this morning (actually I think you said that it was when the congregation was singing, "Here I Am, Lord"), a sense of confirmation swept over you, and suddenly you felt "about 95% sure" that God is calling you to some form of ministry.

Your mother's response was threefold. She said (1) if you're 95% sure, you're as sure as you can ever be with God; (2) nobody but you is likely to be surprised about the fact that God is calling you; and (3) she really wanted at that moment to be able to hug you and not be with me on a visiting professor gig on the other side of the country.

She's right on all counts.

Ninety-five percent! That's more certainty than most of us get when dealing with God. You may find some degree of certainty in mathematics, maybe some in biochemistry and other hard sciences, but you'll never find much in matters of faith and calling. I have a theory that this is why some scientists who convert to Christianity become apologists for Christian fundamentalism — they're searching for a version of Christianity that provides the same level of certainty they expect in their day jobs. But we'll save that conversation for another time.

You may not have seen this vocation coming, but it makes a lot of sense in retrospect. You have an undergraduate degree in political science. You have a master's degree in finance (I wish more ministers had at least a little of this training!). And you've worked in the field of fundraising for nonprofit organizations. All this education and experience, in your mind, was leading toward public service or into politics. In retrospect, however, it all makes sense as a foundation for ministry.

You love politics because you want to make a difference in the world. Much of what you learned in finance and business administration will make you a more knowledgeable leader. And the reason you found fundraising meaningful was because you enjoy developing relationships with people and were committed to the mission of the group you raised money for.

Kierkegaard once said that we have to live our lives forwards, but we can only understand them backwards.[32] I believe this is true. I also believe there's no such thing as wasted experience when it comes to the providence of God. You don't need to regret the fact that you didn't do "pre-theology" in college, or that you didn't recognize or respond to this calling before getting an M.B.A.

You said at one point, "I just want to know what God wants me to do." I still remember what a former president of our seminary, Bob Shelton, said to a senior seminary student one day when she told Bob she just wanted to know what God's will was for her life. Bob said, "God's will for you is to be faithful wherever you are."

If you had a big map of the whole world of your experience, just imagine a huge red dot that says, "YOU ARE HERE." And all you have to do is be faithful right here. But remember, the "YOU ARE HERE" marker keeps moving, because we keep moving, growing, and changing.

I feel honored that you've asked me to help you think further about your calling, and how you will discern it more clearly in the days to come, as you move through seminary. That word you used, "discern," is the right one. Discernment of your calling is the key, and discernment requires that you sharpen your listening skills. Sometimes this means listening to your own gifts and interests, letting your life speak, to use Parker Palmer's wonderful phrase.[33] Sometimes discernment requires listening for God's (sometimes gratingly, annoyingly) "still, small voice" speaking deep inside your heart. And sometimes discernment requires listening to the voices of others through whom God may also be speaking, and these voices may not be saying the same thing your own heart is saying (remember John Calvin?). God moves, they say, in mysterious ways. Well, God speaks in mysterious ways too. It doesn't require a semester of studying Karl Barth's theology to know what Barth knew about this: God and our own humanity are hidden from us even while they are revealed to us in Jesus Christ.

But I would say one more thing. God calls us in ways that correspond to the gifts God has given us, and that means (at least in part) that your interests and passions are not alien issues when it comes to discerning God's calling. Don't forget this! You are intelligent and hardworking: these are gifts that are easy for you to recognize. You are also gentle and tolerant of others: these are gifts that you are only beginning to recognize in yourself. Remain open to God, of course, as you read and pray in response to the Bible; and remain open to the voice of the Holy Spirit as God speaks through other people, especially those people in our congregation and in the larger church as they seek to guide your discernment; but remain open to yourself too, especially the more hidden aspects of yourself, those parts of yourself you may not yet recognize as potential blessings for others.

I know that you haven't fully settled on the direction of your calling. That's fine; you don't have to. The truth is that none of us know all the twists and turns and crossroads our vocations will take in the future. If we did, we might be too scared to move.

When I was eighteen years old, I was sure I would be an evangelist. At twenty-two, I knew I would never serve as a pastor. By the time I was twenty-seven, I was settling into my first call as a pastor and fully expected to serve in congregational ministry for the rest of my life. Today I'm an academic dean of a theological seminary, and have served for the last fifteen years as a professor.

I never saw this coming. But it all makes sense in retrospect. And it will all make sense in retrospect for you too. We just don't know what the "it all" will be yet.

―――――――

Dear Jessica,

I have a bias in favor of thinking. I recognize that. And I find it fascinating that the two friends you mentioned *both* (and for very different reasons) reject the idea that believing in God and thinking can ever really get along.

Your friend the "hardcore atheist," as you say he calls himself, says that it's impossible for "any thinking person" to believe the Christian message because science has displaced all religion. Well, you know I like him a great deal, but his rejection of Christian faith is unthinking. He sounds, in fact, a little like a throwback to the Victorian era to me. His attitude reminds me of a comment by the historian Owen Chadwick, who once wrote, "By 1900 schoolboys decided not to have faith because Science, whatever that was, disproved Religion, whatever that was."[34]

Your other friend, who defines herself as "a strong evangelical Christian," says that her decision not to attend a public university is based on her concern "that *they* will take my faith away from me." I find that whole perspective on faith sad and rather lacking in courage. If your God can't survive sophomore biology, your faith has bigger problems than Charles Darwin! God is not a proposition that needs to be proven, but a personal reality who must be experienced *as a person,* trusted (or distrusted) the way you trust (or distrust) a person. The eighteenth-century philosopher J. G. Hamann argued that God is not a mathematician, but a poet.[35] Anyone who has experienced nature (not the polite, manicured garden variety, but the splendid, dangerous Rocky Mountain sort) can understand what he meant.

Sadly, the wounds that many Christians have endured on the matters of faith and reason, religion and science, are largely self-inflicted. We have spent far too much time trying to argue people into believing, rather than simply living our faith, finding wonder in God's world and awe in the presence of the Creator of this universe, respecting the image of God that God created in every living human being. We don't need to pound people over the head with our Bibles or our experiences of conversion or our morality. As Marilynne Robinson says in her novel *Gilead,* "Nothing true can be said about God from a posture of defense." We need to recover the joy of our salvation — *our* salvation, that simple fact that the thing we most need in life is something we cannot do for ourselves.

I was encouraged recently by something your atheist friend said. He said that he found it hard to reconcile his view that Christianity is unthinking with the fact that he respects intellectually both his grandfather and me. This statement brings to mind something the early Christian thinker Tertullian said: *Certum est, quia impossibile est.* "It is certain, because it is impossible." This is true for me. There are aspects of our faith that we affirm precisely *because* they stretch credulity. This is not irrationality, but a reasonable attempt to come to grips with that mystery that lies at the heart of reality and that enlarges our hopes.

A God capable merely of the possible is not a God big enough to believe in, let alone to hope in. "Nothing can save us that is possible," wrote the poet W. H. Auden. "We who must die demand a miracle."[36] Maybe if your friend grasps the central fact of Christian faith, that we aren't merely trying to account for the difficult or to explain the bewildering, but that we are trusting in One who can do the impossible, that we are pursuing the meaning of ultimate reality beyond the boundaries of human knowledge, then he would be on his way at least to understand the nature and the problem of belief.

Thomas Merton, the writer and Trappist monk, was drawn into the Christian faith in large measure by the power of this very idea. When we speak of God we are speaking of "the vital animating principle of reality — 'pure act,' being itself or per se, existence in perfection, outside of space and time, transcending all human imagery, calmly, steadily, eternally being," as one of his biographers put it. "'What a relief it was for me, now,' [Merton] recalled, 'to discover not only that no idea of ours, let alone any image, could adequately represent God, but also that we should not allow ourselves to be satisfied with any such knowledge of him.'"[37] Our friend Cindy Rigby has a nifty riff on St. Augustine that she uses with her first year theology students; it runs along the same track as Merton's comments: "If you have understood, what you have understood is not God."

This is a message that believers and nonbelievers would do well to heed. I remember, for instance, a student who came to see me after class one day. She said, "You theologians make this God business far too complicated." I answered her by placing my hand on the desk and asking her, "Is this desk solid?" "Of course it is," she said. "I agree, at least in part," I said. "But I am told by physicists that at a subatomic level this desk is in flux, that matter and energy are exchanged in ways we literally cannot conceive of, that this desk is as much in motion as Heraclitus's river.

You know the passage in Heraclitus? 'The river where you set your foot just now is gone — those waters giving way to this, now this.'[38] If my desk is that complicated, if the reality of my desk is hidden from me, isn't it fair to imagine that ultimate reality, the ground of being who created all things and holds all things in existence, is no less complicated?"

I certainly find it no more strange to hear a theologian marvel at the possibility that "God is the infinite sphere whose center is everywhere, whose circumference nowhere," than to hear a physicist like Stephen Hawking discuss the mind-boggling point of absolute singularity.[39] In some sense, people of faith (and that includes theologians) are simply inquiring into that which many others take for granted. As Rumi, the Sufi poet, writes:

> The spirit is so near that you can't see it!
> But reach for it . . . don't be a jar
> Full of water, whose rim is always dry.
> Don't be a rider who gallops all night
> And never sees the horse that is beneath him.[40]

By the way, I really like your disbelieving friend's liveliness. When he disbelieves something, he really gives it his heart and soul. He reminds me of some of the characters that the novelist Graham Greene created who in their spiritual struggles punch and kick and gouge God with the bile and vigor of an Old Testament patriarch, the sort like Jacob who would bite God's ear off if that's what it took to resolve the irresolvable stresses of existence. Give me an aggressively disbelieving atheist any day over either a lukewarm believer or a convinced and unquestioning religionist!

At least the livid atheist is paying attention to the disso-nance of life. Of course, that is one of God's oldest tricks to draw humanity to him. Fish splash hardest when they're hooked! Our hearts are restless, as St. Augustine famously said in his *Confessions,* until they rest in God — and our hearts are likely to be most restless when God's Spirit is striving within us. I will leave your friend's faith in God to God. It sounds like God is working on him.

Have you read any of the new "attacks" on religion by athe-ists concerned about the dangers posed by people who believe in God? While the books and articles have gotten considerable press coverage, on the whole I have found them ironically lack-ing precisely at the level of intellectual engagement.

I was especially disappointed in Christopher Hitchens's *God Is Not Great: How Religion Poisons Everything.* Hitchens is an ele-gant writer, a witty, stimulating, and intelligent journalist, but his critique of faith amounts to little more than a caricature. I saw my old friend Scott Black-Johnston a few days ago. Scott had just read Hitchens's book, largely because, as a pastor, his congregation has been asking lots of questions about it. He ob-served that the book would have been really interesting if Hitchens had taken the faiths he criticizes more seriously. In-stead he preaches largely for the benefit of a choir that already agrees with him. I felt the same way about Richard Dawkins's book, *The God Delusion.* Both writers would do better if they spent some time getting to know their enemy. Dawkins's read-ing of Christian and Hebrew scriptures, for example, pretends to score major points, noting profound contradictions and irra-tionalities that, frankly, have been subject to far more probing reflection and criticism by generations of Christian scholars. Dawkins's approach to the biblical texts seems to assume that people of faith all approach their scriptures with the most naïve and uncritical eyes.

What a pity that these challenges to faith are not better done, because thoughtful critiques of faith and the faithful can be beneficial both for believers and nonbelievers, and they are more necessary today than ever. For Christians, thoughtful challenges to the underlying assumptions of our faith and to our romantic reconstructions of history can help us think and talk about God more honestly, more responsibly, more humbly, and more reverently.

You may recall the story, for example, of how the brilliant philosopher (and student of Ludwig Wittgenstein) Elizabeth Anscombe — a Catholic herself, by the way — undercut the philosophical assumptions C. S. Lewis relied on to justify his belief in miracles. The experience was particularly humiliating for Lewis because it occurred on his home turf in the Socratic Club of Oxford, where Lewis often rationally defended the claims of Christian faith against unbelievers. The experience was doubly humiliating because Lewis's arguments were (to use his own phrase) "demolished" by a Christian. This defeat signaled a crucial change for Lewis. One of his friends said afterward that Lewis had now "lost everything and come to the foot of the cross."[41] From this point on, Lewis turned his energy from writing relatively superficial Christian apologetics to imaginative works, like the Chronicles of Narnia and *Till We Have Faces,* that explore the themes of faith, but in ways that open hearts and minds to undreamed-of possibilities rather than trying to pummel people into believing what we believe.

The fact that Lewis was trounced by a tough-minded Christian who asked critical questions about inadequate theological thinking is especially interesting to me. This week I was enjoying the relative calm between storms in my office by reading, and I came across a small volume of lectures given by Cambridge theologians many years ago on the subject, *Objections to Christian Belief*. One of the scholars noted the value of having those who live astride the boundary of their own Christian faith and the "radical unbelief of the contemporary world" to raise serious objections to our faith. "If there is to be a profound recovery of Christian belief . . . it will surely come out of such an experience."[42]

C. S. Lewis's faith was larger and deeper, and he served others better in their quest for faith, after his superficial arguments for God's existence were jettisoned. Maybe — just maybe — faith is best lived on those various semi-permeable boundaries between faith and doubt, culture and communities of faith, because we as human beings are the ultimate boundary creatures. As Karl Barth said to an audience of German university students right after World War II, "Heaven is the creation inconceivable, earth the creation conceivable. [The human] is the creature on the boundary between heaven and earth."[43]

Dear Jeremy and Jessica,

In the past few days each of you has talked with me about love and marriage, and what it takes for long-term happiness in relationships, so I thought it would make sense to write this letter to both of you. There are few subjects in the world in which the divide between the resources of our faith and the assumptions of our culture differ more profoundly than on the subject of love. Our culture sees love primarily as a feeling. I'm almost tempted to say that our culture sees love as a feeling of dependence.

What I mean can be seen in any greeting card store. Just peruse the romantic section sometime and note how many of the cards give the impression that the sender can't live without the beloved. If dependence is what love is all about, then the ideal of romantic love in our culture is an intestinal parasite that can't survive without its host.

In a slightly different take on love, sometimes popular culture tends to portray it as a feeling of happiness. Thus being "in love" is reduced to feeling pleasure — "you make me happy," or "you're fun to be with."

I'm not knocking romance or fun. In fact, I'm a huge fan of romance, and I think fun is, well, fun. But what I want to call into question is the frightfully shaky foundation for relationships provided by this popular view of love. Incidentally, it's not just shaky because of the prominence of emotion. Emotions, feelings, the whole affection side of life is vital to a rich, full humanity. We are complex creatures that exist physically, emotionally, and spiritually, and all aspects of our humanity, including emotions, need to thrive if we are to be whole. The real problem with the popular concept of love is that it is fundamentally conditional. Whether that conditionality is expressed through the language of dependence or of emotions, its real basis is revealed in statements like "I love you because you . . . (fill in the blank)" or "I will love you if you . . . (fill in the blank)." In either case, the message sent is this: *if you stop providing what I want or need or desire, I will stop loving you.*

As a pastor, I became aware of this dynamic when it became *de rigueur* for couples to write their own marriage vows. Young cou-

74

ples came to me and said they didn't want "the same old vows everyone else uses," they wanted something unique. They wanted to write their own vows. They rejected the classic wedding promises, in other words, not because of what the vows said or didn't say, but because if they were used by others then they must not be "special" or "real." Now, my theology is rooted in the Christian existentialist tradition, and this had the feel of a quest for authenticity about it, so I decided to give couples a chance to write their own vows. In the end I discovered that this whole move to individual vow-writing had less to do with the quest for authenticity than with fashion and the vogues of a burgeoning wedding industry. I came to believe that most couples should never write their own vows because when they do the vows turn into conditional contracts rather than expressions of unconditional covenant. After a year or two I returned to the classical forms and simply gave couples an opportunity, in conversation with me as their pastor, to choose their vows from among the classical forms. In fact, the whole enterprise turned out to be a really good opportunity to reflect with couples on the nature of love. (This was one of the points at which your father discovered that fashion makes a pretty poor motivation for liturgical change.)

Obviously I don't do many weddings these days, having left congregational ministry. But I'm still asked to perform the occasional marriage service for friends and family, and one stands out, not just because of my friendship with the couple (who are also family), but because of the very personal incident surrounding their wedding. This was the wedding, several years ago now, of your cousin Todd to Lisa. The incident involved your mother and me.

Once every two or three hundred years your mother and I have a real argument. You have both remarked that you don't remember us arguing much as you grew up. We certainly disagreed about some things, and we have had our share of arguments, but we always took seriously the importance of modeling how to disagree with humility and openness, how to argue civilly, even when angry. I still remember this particular argument. It was a private matter between us that I will not go into with you even now. But it was painful, and we were in the midst of it during the day or two leading up to Todd and Lisa's wedding. When I presided at the wedding, and preached the very brief wedding homily, it was our marriage, your mom's and mine, not Todd's and Lisa's, that I had in mind, though your mother was the only other person in the congregation who knew it. After reading Ephesians 3:14-21 and Matthew 7:24-25, I preached the following sermon (I hope neither of you minds my sticking a sermon into our correspondence, especially since the sermon repeats two quotes I've already shared with you in these letters!):

What I know about marriage could be written in large print on the back of a matchbox — and maybe that's where it belongs.

Over the past twenty years of ministry I have stood in this spot more times than I can count and led more couples than I can remember through these vows, promises, and prayers. And I have to tell you: What I have learned in counseling and marrying couples is relatively insignificant in comparison to the mysteries of the human heart and the vagaries of human relationships.

Over the past twenty years I have also had the good fortune to be married to the same person, and perhaps she would be the right person to ask what makes marriage work — certainly she knows better than I do. What I have learned from her about marriage is more important than everything I have learned as a theologian and a pastor.

Marriage goes to the very marrow of our bones as human beings.

St. Augustine wrote of God in his *Confessions* that "our hearts are restless until they rest in thee." And there is something of the same reality reflected in marriage: Our hearts are restless until they rest in that other person whose life corresponds to and complements our own, in whose face we find reflected our best face and in whose heart we find a home for our prodigal spirits.

Todd and Lisa, this I know about marriage: This woman — and this man — standing opposite you is not simply an image of the yearning inside of you. She is — and he is — a human being in all the stubborn independence of an other. This will make you crazy sometimes, but it just may save you from yourself, too.

I think this is, in part, why St. Paul speaks of marriage as a reflection of the relationship between Jesus Christ and the Church. Two persons become in marriage one flesh, a single body, a living organism. While the two never cease being two, yet the two truly become one. There is distance and distinction between the two, even in their union. And even though they are distinct and separate from one another, they do become one.

All of us know how painful it is for the whole body when a finger gets smashed in a car door. Likewise in marriage, the whole body can suffer the pains of hellish alienation when one member feels asundered and shut out from the other; and when one member rejoices, the whole body is lifted into that joy. But when the two become so melded and stuck together that they are unable to think and feel on their own, their union can become a kind of oppression. Christ calls us to be human in relationship, and this requires that we learn to embrace but not to cling.

Today we are assembled as a kind of rag-tag and impromptu community of faith, drawn together to celebrate with Lisa and Todd their union. We come together as the church to pray that God the divine Lover will share with them that Love which is a rushing spring with no holding trough beneath, as someone once said. We come to pray that God the Beloved will share with them that perfect grace of receiving and returning love, as is testified by the great traditions of our faith. We come to pray that God's Spirit, who is Love, will breathe life into their marriage, and we are present at the creation. We make these prayers ourselves, for our lives and our marriages also, because this is the common worship of the people of God, and not merely a ceremony in a church building; and these vows which Todd and Lisa make aloud can and should be renewed under our breath as we pray along with them.

This morning we have heard the words of Jesus Christ; let us remember them when we go forth from this place: "Everyone . . . who hears these words of mine and acts on them will be like a wise man who built his house on rock. The rain fell, the floods came and the wind blew on that house, but it did not fall, because it had been founded on rock. And everyone who hears these words of mine and does not act on them will be like a foolish man who built his house on sand. The rain fell, and the flood came, and the winds blew and beat against that house, and it fell — and great was its fall."

These words come at the close of Jesus' Sermon on the Mount, the most wonderful and difficult of Jesus' sayings. The English translation of his words runs to just five pages. But in those five pages, Jesus reverses almost everything we might describe as "good advice." And I think there's a warning here. What we need this morning as we worship together, what Todd and Lisa need, is not good advice, but good news. We need to hear the Good News.

I once asked an elderly widow what was the secret to marriage. Her marriage had been legendary in the town where we lived. She and her late husband had lived for years a life of mutual support and friendship, raising two terrific children. I expected her to talk about lofty things like the depth of their love. She surprised me. She said the secret of marriage is to learn to forgive. I'm not sure I understood then. I think I'm beginning to understand, though.

On some days, maybe most days, amid the ordinariness and busy-ness of life, love is too flighty and abstract a word to use. To say, "I love you," can almost sound like a threat or a curse or a refusal to face the tough realities of living together. But to learn to forgive, to learn to leave judgment with God, this may be the wisdom of marriage. And it is what Jesus tells us to build our houses on: "Do not judge, so that you may not be judged. For with the judgment you make you will be judged, and the measure you give will be the measure you get. Why do you see the speck in your wife's eye, but do not notice the log in your own? Or how can you say to your husband, 'Let me take that speck out of your eye,' while ignoring the log in your own eye? First take the log out of your own eye, and then you will see clearly how to help your spouse."

Perhaps this is what Søren Kierkegaard meant when he said that we should be completely objective in looking at ourselves and entirely subjective in dealing with others. Or perhaps C. S. Lewis was getting at this when he told us that God's wisdom in relationships is the very opposite of ours: We say to understand is to forgive; God says to forgive is to understand.

So I say to you, Todd and Lisa, and to us all: Let us hear the good news that makes it possible for us to live together as one flesh without getting under each other's skin. There will be days when love seems a grand and lofty abstraction and understanding the behavior of those with whom we live may seem an impossible goal, but let us always forgive one another, that we may be forgiven. "Everyone then who hears these words . . . and acts on them will be like a wise person who built his house on the rock." Amen.

When I turned to the bride and groom that morning, after offering this meditation, I took the set of vows they had chosen from the *Book of Common Prayer* and led them in these unconditional promises:

In the Name of God I take you to be my wife (my husband) to have and to hold from this day forward, for better for worse, for richer for poorer, in sickness and in health, to love and to cherish, until we are parted by death. This is my solemn vow.

It occurs to me that sometimes it's the simplest things in our Christian tradition that are the most profound and revolutionary: a helpless infant is baptized in the name of God, and in this act the Church proclaims that God claims this child in grace even before the child has the capacity to reach out and make any claim on God. We lower the dead body of someone we love into the ground with the unprecedented expectation that God will recreate that person from the dust even as God originally created the dust from nothing. A couple stand facing one another pledging that they will remain faithful to one another come hell or high water, and that no future circumstance will change their commitment to love, cherish, and forgive one another. And in all of these things we are saying: God is like this. God accepts us without condition. God creates and recreates us out of nothing. God remains faithful in the midst of all our shortcomings, redeeming our lives from every pit into which we fall.

But the fact that love is an act of grace doesn't mean that love is effortless. Love takes work, but that's not the same as saying that love is toil and drudgery. Take care as you prepare to enter into the relationship with another person to whom you want to give yourself unconditionally. Play is involved in any kind of work worth doing. Otherwise, the love is not worthy of the name love. Children know this is true, that's why their play is their work and their work is their play. And no one knows how to love better and more truly than a child.

By the way, something else happened at Todd and Lisa's wedding that I just remembered this morning. It may be illuminating.

Most wedding photographers with whom I've worked are conscientious. Most are sensitive to the fact that a Christian wedding is a service of worship, not simply a social event. Most photographers recognize this and work with the minister, understanding that the pastor is responsible to ensure the integrity of the service as the worship of God. Well, the photographer for this particular wedding was neither terribly sensitive nor conscientious. He was also pretty manipulative. During the rehearsal he and I went over the details about where the video camera could be set up and what flash photographs would be allowed during the actual service, but every time I turned around he found a way to forget what we had agreed.

On the morning of the wedding, when I went into the sanctuary to go over the details one last time with the church's wedding coordinator, the photographer was setting up a tripod with a flash camera on it directly behind the Communion Table where I was to stand facing the couple. And when I told him that the camera is not permitted there because it distracts the worshipers from the liturgy, he went ballistic. After he calmed down, I instructed him to remove his gear, and to return to the place where we had agreed he could take all the photos he wanted.

Muttering, he removed his gear. A few minutes later, he made his way to the back of the sanctuary where a good-looking blue-eyed brunette was sitting in a pew. The photographer struck up a conversation with her, hoping he had found a listener as sympathetic as she was attractive. After relating his difficulties, he told her, "That preacher is a real sonofabitch!" To which she responded, "You're not telling me anything. I'm married to that sonofabitch."

Dear Jessica,

A few days ago a student told me that she was troubled by a friend who when she prays invokes God's presence using all sorts of sacred names. She prays to God the Father, Son, and Holy Spirit; Creator, Sustainer, and Wisdom; Elohim, Yahweh, Christ; and even, because she was brought up in a predominantly Buddhist country, refers to God using terms that derive from that faith, the faith to which her parents still belong.

The student asked me if it was wrong to do this. I told her that I use the vocabulary of Christian faith because that is the particular "way" given to me to enter the life of the Spirit in the household of humankind. When I pray, I draw on the piety of Judaism and Christianity because these are the given terms of my faith tradition. I pray to the God and Father of our Lord Jesus Christ, to the God of Abraham, Isaac, and Jacob. I pray to the Creator, Redeemer, and Sustainer; the Father, Son, and Holy Spirit. Indeed, when my prayer language reflects the faith recorded in the Old Testament, where other wonderfully descriptive terms for God emerge, I pray to God as Lord Sabaoth (the Lord of hosts), Adonai or Kurios (both of which mean Lord, the former in Hebrew and the latter in Greek), El Shaddai (God Almighty). All of these ways of speaking to God or appealing to God or invoking God's presence have made their way into the Christian faith. Our faith gives us many, many more ways to call upon God, to speak to and to speak about God.

When I think about calling on God in prayer, there are two things I don't want to forget, however.

First, the holy, hidden, sacred name of God is YHWH. We don't even have the vowels to speak this name because to the ancient Hebrews it was too sacred to utter. Those who, in the Christian tradition, say that God's *name* is "Father, Son, and Holy

Spirit," and that this is the only name by which we can speak of God, are, theologically, simply inaccurate. They are wrong not because they are impious, but, ironically, because their pious anxiety over orthodoxy leads them to say something that is Christianly untrue. The Trinitarian formula, "Father, Son, and Holy Spirit," describes a relationship, the holy mystery of God's intra-relatedness, the holy mystery of the plurality-in-unity that lies at the heart of God's "who-ness" (to use a theological term that sounds like it comes straight from Dr. Seuss, but really comes from ancient Orthodox patristic writers like Gregory of Nyssa and Basil of Caesarea).

Second, to invoke God's presence is dangerous business, and we should never take the act of invocation lightly or for granted. Worship is not a parlor game. Worship is not a form of entertainment. Worship is not a convention of the like-minded. Worship is a corporate work of paying attention to God, invoking God's presence, offering our sacrifices of praise and thanksgiving in and through the Spirit of Christ who intercedes for us, recognizing our sin and asking for God's forgiveness even as we pledge ourselves to forgive others as freely as we are forgiven, praying for the needs of others and bringing our resources together to relieve their needs, and marshaling to go forth into the world in the name of Jesus to extend to others the peace with which God has blessed us. This is serious business.

So I stick close to the tradition passed down to me when I worship and pray. But this does not mean that others, whose traditions are different from mine and whose faith is fed by streams that are well beyond my knowledge and experience, are not being honest to God when they don't pray as I pray! It is an awesome thing to fall into the hands of a living God. And there's an appropriate theological agnosticism essential to reverence that keeps me from condemning the prayers of others, even as it holds me accountable to pray with longing and love (yes, of course), but also with fear and trembling. This theological agnosticism need not extend as far as a character in a Robin Jenkins novel takes it when he says, "I've got too much respect for God to believe in Him."[44] But it should be thorough enough to make us sense the absoluteness of the boundary between the Eternal (God's realm) and the created (including us).

I'm reminded of something Annie Dillard once wrote about the Hasidic rabbi who "refused to promise a friend to visit him the next day: 'How can you ask me to make such a promise? This evening I must pray and recite 'Hear, O Israel.' When I say these words, my soul goes out to the utmost rim of life. . . . Perhaps I shall not die this time either, but how can I now promise to do something at a time after the prayer?'"[45]

You mentioned to me recently how much you enjoyed reading C. S. Lewis's *Till We Have Faces*. You know how much I love that book too — I think it may be Lewis's best achievement. Do you remember the old priest's description of God in that novel? The old priest is criticizing those who want a simple, transparent, utterly rational, understandable and ultimately controllable God. They do not understand "holy things," the old priest says to his king. "They demand to see such things clearly, as if the gods were no more than letters written in a book. I, King, have dealt with the gods for three generations of men, and I know that they dazzle our eyes and flow in and out of one another like eddies on a river, and nothing that is said clearly can be said truly about them. Holy places are dark places. It is life and strength, not knowledge and words, that we get in them. Holy wisdom is not clear and thin like water, but thick and dark like blood."[46]

The ancient temple, in which the old priest served, as you will remember, was dark within, and the aroma of blood, the blood of countless sacrifices, could not be disguised or washed from its floors and walls.

If there is any feature of contemporary Christian faith in North America that I find lacking it is our failure to sense awe in the presence of the Holy. Maybe it is related to our alienation from the dark skies at night where once upon a time we glimpsed the Milky Way even from suburban homes, but now we see only the reflected light of parking lots and malls and streetlamps. I don't know why we fail to sense what any rational being should in the presence of the ultimate boundaries, the boundaries of transcendence, of being itself, of life beyond life and death beyond death, but God is frequently treated as just another constituency to be enlisted in our latest causes, an infinite cipher waiting to be filled with our values and views. All the while, we avoid the testimony of the centuries of faith that bear witness in awe-full silence before they stammer a single word in confession, and adamantly refuse to equate God's ways with our ways. Approaching this boundary, the boundary between God and us, all the other great boundaries of existence, such as the boundary between non-being and existence, shrink to insignificance. Even the boundary of death itself, as Toni Morrison says in her novel *Beloved,* "is a skipped meal compared to this."[47]

With what words can we speak? What names ought we to use? With what terrible hesitance should we proceed until the words and names are compelled by God to come from our lips?

The fact that God draws near to us in Jesus Christ does not lessen God's transcendence, God's otherness. Close proximity only makes the holiness of the Holy more obvious. When Moses brushed by the *mysterium tremendum,* when he was startled into submission by the consciousness of the immediacy of the holy God, his humanity seemed to teeter on the brink of extinction: what can we say when even shrubbery spontaneously bursts into flames in God's presence? When the ancient high priests of Israel went into the Holy of Holies to offer sacrifice for the people's sins before the Ark of the Covenant, reputedly they had a rope tied around one leg so that at least their bodies could be recovered should the presence of God kill them. But many religious people seem to want a domesticated God, a tamed God, and they think they've found one in Jesus Christ because he reveals God's love to us on the cross. I wonder if they are paying attention to the cross at all.

Yes, there's the love of God revealed on the cross, but revealed in suffering and terror, in the execution of an innocent man, the complicity of every conceivable earthly power, and the seeming impotence of the all-powerful Creator of the universe, his Father in heaven. You and Jeremy loved Lewis's story *The Lion, the Witch and the Wardrobe* when you were children. I wish more contemporary Christians understood the distinction that Mr. Beaver made between Aslan, the great lion who symbolizes Jesus, being safe (which Aslan most certainly wasn't) and Aslan being good (which he most definitely was).

Idolatry, the fashioning of gods in our own image, is such a subtle danger today for Christians. Perhaps it is for all religious people; perhaps it always has been such a danger. In any case, it goes way beyond just treating Jesus as our "best buddy," and includes the search for ever more titillating religious experiences (more smoke, bigger mirrors), the vapid worshiper descending into a spiral of spiritual pornography before the naked image of the self enlarged to the dimensions of infinity and called God.

God withheld his name from Jacob the night they wrestled

beside the river. God blessed Jacob, but God refused to be manipulated by a master manipulator. So when people pray, I can imagine them reaching out in their stammering human words, uttering names they hope against hope will invoke God's presence, bearing witness to the greatness of God and the limitations of their human understanding, sometimes reverently and appropriately trying to touch the hem of the garment of the Holy, and sometimes trying to grasp God and not let God go until they are blessed. Perhaps there is a fine line between invocation and manipulation. Perhaps this is all inevitable.

What is specifically forbidden, of course, in the Ten Commandments is to take the name of God in vain, which has nothing to do with "cussing" and everything to do with using God's name "in the pursuit of nothingness."[48] I fear that too many religious people today make precisely this error. We take God's name in vain whenever we empty God's name of holiness (of sacredness, otherness, and transcendence) so as to manipulate God for our own ends — for instance, when we try to use God's authority as the definitive conversational trump card or as the means to an end (whether the end is social, cultural, political, economic, or religious). God is simply too big to be contained by anything we can construct, even our prayers.

Even Jesus of Nazareth, when he prayed, followed the intimate invocation, "Our Father," with the recognition of God's holiness, "Hallowed be thy name." Strangely enough, this may be a fact an observant and attentive agnostic comprehends better than many deeply pious Christians.

Dear Jeremy,

I'm not sure I remember exactly the way you asked your question a few days ago, but it was something to the effect, "How can I be sure I'm heading in the right direction when I'm trying to follow God's leadership?" I know I responded then by talking about discernment, and by sharing the words of two different theologians with you. But I thought I would take another stab at responding to you, because the more I think about discerning God's will, the more complex the questions become. What I want to share with you today is both theological and very personal.

After you left the house last night, I was reading the Sunday *New York Times,* and I came across an obituary for the theologian John Macquarrie. I had heard from some British colleagues recently that Macquarrie was quite ill. The news of his death left me sad and deeply grateful for the things I learned from his writings over the years.

The writer of the obituary in the *Times* quoted a reviewer as saying, "unlike some modern theologians, John Macquarrie writes about God as though he believes in him." Indeed, Macquarrie did believe in God. But he could still baffle the pious, especially when he said things like, "Faith's name for reality is God."[49] A person of Christian faith, according to Macquarrie, has a different perspective on existence than people who do not believe. A Christian believes that existence is good because he believes that God's Being upholds everything that exists, and the God who upholds all things has revealed himself as good in Jesus Christ.

For theologians of my generation, Macquarrie was one of those sensible, believing elder voices that helped us find a vigorous and vital Christian faith amid the rubble and rancor of the late twentieth century. Today as I rambled through his books, I came across a dog-eared page marred by underlining galore. And I thought again about your question, and about your quest for God's direction in your life:

> Belief that there is a real river flowing outside of my window is confirmed by everyone who looks out and sees it; but there is no such universal agreement about the reality of God, and no simple way of testing the belief, like looking out of the window. . . . It is part of the meaning of the word "faith" that there cannot be certitude in these matters. Faith is not sight, and so to live in faith is to live with the possibility that the faith may be an illusion, in the sense that it refers to nothing beyond one's own states of mind.[50]

Here's where all this connects with your question: the best we can do as we seek to discern God's direction for our lives is to trust that God created us and set us in the midst of the flow of life, and that as life's courses change and situations shift, the gifts God has given us will be called upon in new and varied ways. We cannot know ahead of time how or where or how fast the stream will be moving, but we can trust ourselves to it with the confidence that the God who has placed us here has given us ways and means to respond. The confidence, however, must be balanced with the humility that what we believe may be illusory, and we must be open to test our perspective against the perceptions of others. Macquarrie wasn't writing about vocation when he wrote these words, but there is a nice echo in the room.

I don't know where or to what God is calling you. But I am grateful that you understand your vocation as a calling and not just a career. You have mentioned to me several times the difference you've seen in friends who pursue a vocation rather than those who just get jobs, even lucrative jobs.

I'm thinking, for instance, of your old school friend John, and how much he loves being a chef. I would never have imagined John as a chef when you and he were in high school and college. It's amazing how his purpose and zeal for life were waiting for him in his calling. I know you've been frustrated, bouncing from one position to another since graduating from college, moving from fundraising to sales, using bits of your finance and administration training first in this job, then in another, waiting, but not knowing for sure what you are waiting for. The calling you are experiencing, which is moving you now to seminary, stirs up the vocational questions more than it settles them. This is as appropriate as it is disturbing. Faith is funny this way — or maybe it's not so funny.

———————

Dear Jessica,

The fact that your own long-term struggle of the soul isn't directly related to any concern over (as the phrase goes) "life after death" is on the whole a positive thing, at least in my view. Your concern is with the truth of the matter: Is there a God? What might be the character of God if God exists? How would one know God? If God exists what does God want of us? You have asked questions about the nature of ultimate reality, about meaning for life in general and you in particular. You haven't been all that concerned with the issue of life after death. This is certainly consistent with your usual way of tackling issues. You'd rather know what the truth is first, then adjust your feelings to that. Your concern isn't particularly self-serving.

On top of that, you're in good company. C. S. Lewis in *Surprised by Joy* says that his own coming to faith was unrelated in any way to any preoccupation with "a future life." While Lewis is generous to those Christians who have made "immortality" the core doctrine of their religion, he maintains that a "preoccupation with that subject," particularly at the outset of one's faith journey, could hardly "fail to corrupt the whole thing."[51] Likewise John McLeod Campbell, the extraordinary Scottish theologian, writing a century before Lewis, called into question the reduction of Christian faith to fire insurance. Campbell believed that for many people faith in Christ had been utterly misinterpreted as yet another attempt to preserve their lives (something Jesus specifically condemned). For Campbell, to have eternal life is to share the same life and love of God that is revealed in Jesus Christ, who lived and died for others. Indeed, to have eternal life is to share the Holy Spirit of God that is the very Life and Love that God the Father shares with God the Son eternally and that filled and motivated the whole life of Jesus of Nazareth when he walked the earth. "God is preparing," Campbell explained, "a family of sons and daughters, to be his companions throughout eternity, who shall be capable of entering into His mind and feelings, and thus have the reality of adoption, the spirit of children."[52]

To love God is not to love what God can do for us. To love God is not to treasure the benefits God can deliver us. Loving God, in other words, is not just a religious version of self-interest and self-preservation. To love God is to delight in God *as God*.

It is especially appropriate that your quest for faith is about the *reality* of God and *relationship* with God, rather than the kind of quest which was more common in the revivalism of my childhood and youth, which was mostly concerned with escaping everlasting punishment ("turn or burn" theology!). I can't tell you how many times we got "saved" when we were kids — virtually every time a new traveling evangelist came to town. And it was usually on Friday night of the revival week that the evangelist saw his biggest altar call, after preaching on the second coming of Jesus, the division of sheep and goats, and the everlasting consignment of goats to hellfire and damnation. (Someday I really must try to find out why goats are so abhorrent to God. Other than their smelling funny, I just don't see the offense!)

Anyway, your quest for faith has not centered on the relative climate of your everlasting destination, and I am grateful for that. And yet you have had a healthy curiosity about death and whether anything comes after. Your questions over the years have frequently reflected this interest.

The first thing I would want to say is that Christian faith assumes that we shall live, and Christian faith affirms that we shall die. I was surprised a couple of years ago, while teaching a class on the theology of death and resurrection, at the answer some students gave when I asked them, "What is the Christian belief about death?" Several students immediately replied, "Christianity does not believe that we shall die."

In fact, nothing could be further from the truth! Christianity consistently has affirmed that we shall all die, and that we shall rot or otherwise decompose. Christianity has confessed perplexity on the question of whether there is a soul *separable* from the body (Christian faith is heir to the faith of Israel that strongly affirms a body-soul unity in distinction from the Greek philosophies that split us up into body-soul or body-mind dichotomies, and Christians have struggled in various ways with the conflict between these spiritual worldviews); but Christianity's hope for the resurrection of the dead in Christ only makes sense against the backdrop of the fact that we believe we shall surely die.

(By the way, I have long suspected that the popularity of the idea of the notion of a Rapture among Dispensationalist Christians is at least partially motivated by a desire to avoid death altogether. I'm acrophobic, as you know, so frankly I would rather die than fly. If the Dispensationalists turn out to be right about the rapture, I truly hope I am long dead by then and sleep through the whole thing.)

Christian faith affirms our commonality with all people in trying to make sense of death as an undeniable and unambiguous boundary that marks the end of our existence as creatures. Life ends. We die. We go the way of all flesh.

For this reason I find the ancient Epic of Gilgamesh deeply comforting. I think you probably know that I read it once a year. This year I'm reading it in a weekly prayer group with seminary students (along with praying the Psalms daily, as usual). It's one of the oldest texts in existence today — something in the neighborhood of four thousand years old. But for me its most striking feature is not its antiquity; rather, it's the way it reads my own heart, the way it grapples with the human business of coming to terms with life and death and the meaning of it all. We're in this thing called life together, it seems to say, and the only way out is through a hole in the ground (or its functional equivalent).

Gilgamesh, the hero of the story, faces the most solemn reality of every human life — it ends. And he faces this reality in the most ordinary and moving way — he witnesses, grieves over, and wrestles with the meaning of the death of his closest friend, Enkidu. Gilgamesh says something like this (please bear with me, I'm quoting from memory!): *My friend, the friend I love so much, who shared every hardship with me, my friend Enkidu, whom I loved so much, is overcome with the fate of all mortals. I was so afraid, afraid of death, that I roamed the country. Am I not like Enkidu? Must I not lie down in death also, never to rise up from this sleep?*

Some people try to comfort Gilgamesh and others try to shame him out of his grief by talking about the inevitability of death and death's invisible hand reaching across all lands and into every family. But Gilgamesh will not be comforted or shamed. He gives himself over to his grief with abandon, like he gives himself over to life itself, and he lets his grief serve as the engine for his inquiry into meaning. Gilgamesh is the first great pilgrim, the first great seeker, and his sorrow-driven quest drives him to try to understand all that a human being can about life and death. If it is true, as a character in *Shadowlands,* the play about C. S. Lewis and Joy Davidman Lewis, says, that we read to remember we are not alone, then Gilgamesh is the most wonderful of texts because it reminds every reader that we humans have always been in this thing called life together, that we are never alone, that there is always another pilgrim, another seeker, beside us searching also to understand what it means to face the boundary of death.[53]

The opening words of Charles Dickens's *A Christmas Carol* come to mind when I think about the human honesty with which Christian faith surveys death. "Old Marley was dead, to begin with. There is no doubt whatever about that. The register of his burial was signed by the clergyman, the clerk, the undertaker, and the chief mourner. Scrooge signed it. And Scrooge's name was good for anything he chose to put his hand to. Old

Marley was as dead as a door-nail. . . . There is no doubt that Marley was dead. This must be distinctly understood, or nothing wonderful can come of the story I am to relate."[54] If Christian faith were put into a novel form it might begin similarly: "We shall all die. If this is not understood then nothing wonderful can come from this story."

Nearly thirty years ago, when I was a middler in seminary and a chaplain intern in a large urban medical center, this understanding broke in upon me at an intimate and personal level. In the surreal world of an intensive care unit, I became pastor to a woman — I'll call her Doris. I sat beside her bed and prayed with her as her internal organs failed one after another. I still remember seeing the phrase "necrotic bowel" somewhere on a chart: dead bowels, dying inside. One night I came up the back stairs and ducked into her room, looking routinely to see the weak smile she always seemed to manage. But there was nothing on her face to read. She'd lapsed into a coma, which became a persistent vegetative state. She declined steadily, systems continuing to fail. Some time later, I can't remember how many weeks, a nurse called to ask me to stand by while the life support system was unplugged. The nurse and I prayed the Lord's Prayer, and I held Doris's cold hand while the monitor went flat. I had never seen someone die before, and not just "someone," someone I knew, someone I served as pastor.

Our supervisor had arranged that same week for all of the chaplain interns to visit the lair of the medical pathologist deep in the bowels of the hospital. "He's just like Quincy," the supervisor said, alluding to a character on a detective show that was popular at the time. "He says his diagnoses are always right; it's just that they come too late." Pathologist as latter-day Cassandra!

We descended into the morgue, where we were to observe an

autopsy. Frightened — much more than merely apprehensive — we inched slowly up around a stainless steel table on which lay a body under a sheet. The pathologist read from a chart with clinical detachment: Woman. 53 years old. 114 pounds. Caucasian. Cause of death: multiple organ failure." Then he said, "Let's see why she really died, boys."

When he pulled back the sheet, I had to gasp. It was not just a 53-year-old Caucasian woman weighing 114 pounds. It was Doris. "She had a name," I thought, angry at the doctor's detachment, angry at seeing her *like this*. The body of this modest woman lay naked before us — six young male seminary students and a male doctor. "She must be cold," I remember thinking, irrationally, remembering that Doris was always cold, always needing another blanket when she was in the ICU. The doctor proceeded to slice and saw Doris open. And I shall never forget his prying apart her rib cage and his words, stark, naked, impersonal, cold words: "We all look like this, fellows: spare ribs just beneath the skin."

Walking into our apartment that night, I must have looked more tired than usual. Your mom asked me how it had gone, and I told her. I felt like something had broken inside me. And I knew that I could never again look at death and the hope for the resurrection of the dead in quite the same way, not after knowing and caring for Doris, not after seeing her and seeing us all as meat, nameless, cold, lying out on a table in a morgue.

Thomas Lynch, a very wise and often funny writer (he's a poet-undertaker, and that's one hyphenated word I never expected to see), quotes worldly-wise La Rochefoucauld as saying, "Death and the sun are not to be looked at in the face."[55] Yet Christianity does look death in the face, with compassion, and sympathy, and sorrow, and regret, and hope. Which brings us to the wonderful thing we miss unless we really do say we shall die: Christians believe not in survival after apparent demise, nor even in the immortality of some shadowy spiritual consciousness or soul after the mortal container bites the dust, but in the resurrection of the dead in Christ.

You have asked me on a couple of occasions if I believe in the resurrection. I have answered you by placing myself in the hands of the oldest creed in Christendom, the Nicene Creed: "I look for the resurrection of the dead." The challenge here is to get your theological analogies right. You see, many people think that resurrection is "like," or analogous to, resuscitating a dead or apparently dead body. Thus every situation from the biblical story of Lazarus to restoring to life a child who has fallen through the ice in a skating accident becomes an analogy for resurrection. In fact, as amazing as it is to resuscitate an apparently dead person or as apparently miraculous as it was to bring Lazarus back from the dead, neither of these kinds of incidents gets at the utterly impossible and unprecedented possibility of which the creed speaks. The analogy of resurrection is not resuscitation, but creation. This is why the whole debate about cremation and burial among some Christians misses the point. Resurrection is not about restoring a body to life, but creating a body out of nothing. But, in this case, the body created out of nothing has continuity with the body that existed before death. And so Paul plays theological Twister for page after page with the Corinthians, and theologians ever after have painted themselves into logical corners, and I am not smart enough to do anything but throw up my hands and say, "I look for the resurrection of the dead." And I do. "I look for the resurrection of the dead, and the life of the world to come."

I do not find belief in the resurrection easy — but nor should

I. Belief in the resurrection, perhaps, should be as impossible as resurrection itself. What I mean by this is simply to say that resurrection is utterly beyond the realm of possibility. Resurrection belongs to the realm of genuine miracle (a word that gets thrown around today so carelessly by the pious and impious alike as to be virtually synonymous with the merely amazing). Belief in the resurrection is granted to us by the God of resurrection who takes our tiny hopes into his hands and refashions them into something beyond all expectation, something inconceivable, impossible, incredible. But, having said this, I do not find belief in the resurrection any more or less possible, any more or less probable, than belief in the creation of the world that now is.

Creation has never stopped taking my breath away. And if you can believe that everything that exists was created out of nothing (creation *ex nihilo* is the theological phrase), then believing that God can create again everything out of nothing is a piece of cake. Resurrection is a second creation, a new creation, quite as inconceivable as creation in the first place.

This does not mean that death's sting is entirely removed, however, even for Christians. On this point I confess some tension with St. Paul when he asks his rhetorical questions: "O death, where is your victory? O death, where is your sting?" (1 Corinthians 15:55). We may not feel the sting of death when we think about our own deaths. But death stings us still when we think of the death of those we love, because we do suffer loss. Perhaps Paul did understand this. He does affirm the fact that we grieve. We just don't grieve like those people who have no hope.

Do you remember the day you and I drove from Austin to Lufkin to visit your great grandmother as she lay dying? The family had called me in to discuss whether we should tell her that she was dying. The doctor had met with the family, and left it to them whether to tell her. So you and I drove home, along the way enjoying one of those glorious and sweet moments in the eye of a storm of impending sorrow. I still recall our singing together with Aretha Franklin that day, and I think our rendition of "(You Make Me Feel Like) a Natural Woman" remains one of the best I've ever heard.

As the family gathered solemnly in the hallway of the hospital, debating whether to tell your great grandmother that she was dying, you sat beside her bed talking with her. Later that day you told me what you talked about. (How old were you then? I don't remember. Maybe twelve or thirteen?) You told me later that you asked her, "Grandmother, do you know you are dying?" And she said, "I know, honey." You said, "But they're all out in the hall discussing whether to tell you." "I know," she said. "It's hard for them."

It was hard for us to let go of someone who had loved us and cared for us for as long as any of us could remember.

My last long visit with your great grandmother (and it was almost a year after the family decided not to tell her she was dying), as she lay in her bed at the nursing home, she asked me to hug her. I did. And as I held her, and we both wept, she said, "I hate this dying. Being dead won't be so bad, but I hate this dying, honey. I'm afraid of dying." "I am too," I said.

And, I think, for both of us the fear of dying has nothing to do with either "faith" or "religion." Maybe it has something to do with what Miguel de Unamuno said: "As human beings we live together, but each of us dies alone, and death is the most extreme solitude."[56] Maybe that is why we both needed to hold on to one another just a little longer. And maybe that's why families and friends gather together after a death even when they don't know what to say to each other, even when all they can do is stare at each other, or crack bad jokes, or drink and eat and stay up too late. We just need to be together to endure the sense of this "most extreme solitude."

You once asked me, "What happens when we die?" I think I would have to say now, "We let go."

It's strange to say this, because the whole "doctrine" of "letting go" has sort of been the key to my understanding of faith all along, but I have never related it to death and resurrection until this very moment, writing you just now. At its heart, faith is a matter of learning to let go, to entrust ourselves to God. When we die, we really do let go. This is what philosopher Emmanuel Levinas means when he (echoing the ancient Greek philosopher Epicurus) writes: "When death is here, I am no longer here, not just because I am nothingness, but because I am unable to grasp."[57]

Like a tiny infant, unable to hold on even to her mother's finger, unable to grasp and pull ourselves, we let go when death is here, and in letting go we are tacitly entrusting all we are to God for whatever may come.

I look for a new creation, which is just another way to say, I look for the resurrection of the dead. If it weren't impossible, it wouldn't be worth hoping.

Dear Jeremy,

I'm so grateful to have had those days with you as we made our way from Texas to New Jersey, and I wouldn't trade anything for the privilege of helping you move into your room at the seminary. It's funny how necessity graces us sometimes. The simple need to get you and your stuff to school provided us with the extravagant blessing of spending five days together. I can't remember the last time I enjoyed anything so much, and I am grateful to your mother for her generosity in allowing us to do this, just us guys, though I know she wanted so much to be with us. Taking turns driving the car; talking about everything under the sun, from the relative merits of Buddy Guy, Jimi Hendrix, Eric Clapton, and Stevie Ray Vaughn to the challenges of Hebrew grammar; tasting barbecue in Memphis and sampling foie gras in Manhattan. It was all fun. So was the side trip we took to the battlefield at Gettysburg. I had never had a sense of what the Civil War historian Shelby Foote was talking about when he described the hand-to-hand combat in this battle until we went through the "Devil's Den" ourselves and saw where the Union line stood face-to-face with the Confederate one. These men were firing literally into each other's faces at point-blank range. I cannot grasp the courage it took for them to do what they did.

It seems to me that courage and fear, anxiety and our responses to it, flavor most every aspect of our lives together from the mundane to the extraordinary. The only moment of tension we experienced in that whole trip was, I now realize in retrospect, because of my own anxiety. I know now that it must have hurt you that I gave you a lecture on how important it is to get a good picture taken for the school's "face book." I went on too long about it, and blew it up too much. You told me that you'd take care of it, and that should have ended the conversation, but

I kept on lecturing well beyond the point when the point was made. Why did I do that?

I'm not sure I know all the levers that operate my own anxieties. But I do know that it is anxiety that made me react. I'm grateful to you that we were able to sort through the tension, and that we were able to move on. You extended grace to me.

After I got home I happened to read a poem by Louise Glück in which she explores how her love for her son does not measure up to the love she hoped she would have toward him. She wanted to love him generously, with an expansive openness toward his freedom, but, she says, like her own mother loved her, she loves him as though he were a flower she is viewing through a magnifying glass, focusing the intense rays of the sun on the grass around him until the grass is scorched and dead.[58]

I hope — I pray — that I love you in your freedom as a person and as a child of God. I think our relationship has good roots, a solid foundation, for friendship and trust, and I'll try not to turn the magnifying glass on you!

You and I have talked about this many times, but the relationship between fathers and sons (as between all parents and children) echoes from one generation to another. You have helped me grow in my relationship with my dad in ways you know about, and in some ways you do not know.

Several years ago, for example, when my dad and I were going through a rough patch, I remember a conversation with a close friend. I complained about something my father had said or done (I can't even remember now what it was), and my friend said, "You know, you really need to work this out with your dad. You love Jeremy and Jessica too much not to have a good relationship with your father." He was right. Dad and I did sort through whatever was going on then, and we have built a stronger, better relationship over the years. I am so grateful now that we did that hard work, because I feel that you and I can talk about virtually anything.

Someone asked me the other day what is the best stage of parenting. I said I've enjoyed them all — so far. But I think the best is friendship, the stage we've reached now, when mutual respect, trust, and freedom characterize a relationship between two adults.

This relationship between two adults is, however, subject to the sometimes unexpected tectonic aftershocks of the accumulated years. I confess to you that I was surprised at the waves of emotion I felt when I stood on the train platform in Princeton getting ready to return home without you.

Suddenly, standing beside you on that platform, twenty-some years collapsed like one of those collapsible drinking cups we used to carry on camping trips, and my memory flashed back to you walking up the steps of the kindergarten. I swear, Jeremy, that it was yesterday that you were five years old, and all the years in between were nanoseconds shooting by at the speed of light. We've seen you graduate from high school, college, and graduate school. We've seen you enter the professional world, live on your own, take responsibility for your own life. Your mother and I have packed your cars and moving vans, time and time again, and yet this time, *this* time, I was emotionally blown away. I didn't expect it. I didn't see it coming.

The other day I joked with Jessica about how I felt when she got her driver's license, that strange feeling of sympathy for the Creator who creates that which is independent from and perhaps dangerous to his own being and the existence of others. But there's another side to creation, and there's another side to parental love. You know as a parent from the very first moment you hold your son or daughter in the hospital that the day will come when you cannot hold on to them, that holding on to them is holding them back, and that you have to let go if you really love them.

Maybe I had never fully understood that before. Maybe every other "letting go" of you had seemed somehow an interim arrangement. And maybe, also, I felt something akin to sacrifice, something terrible and ultimate — something hard to define and harder still to articulate emotionally — in knowing that your future, that your life and calling, is in the hands of a living God.

One of the most awful stories in the Bible is the story of Abraham and Isaac. I continue to be shocked by the fact that most seminary students and many pastors who exegete the passage — Genesis 22, in which God comes to Abraham and demands that he sacrifice his beloved son, Isaac, and Abraham takes his son to the mountain with the full intention of slaying him as a sacrifice to God — do not react in horror to this text. There may be many wonderful insights in this biblical passage, but if we do not first and foremost see it as an occasion of genuine terror, betrayal, fanatical devotion, and unutterable horror, a scene deserving of disgust and repulsion, then we have not heard the text as real, but only as a token, make-believe fable, the ultimate fractured fairytale. Even Kierkegaard's profound retellings of the tale somehow sanitize it, make it safer, though it is Kierkegaard who makes the wise observation, "Abraham I cannot understand, in a certain sense there is nothing I can learn from him but astonishment."[59]

I recall Elie Wiesel's handling of this text, in which he remembers a midrash in which Abraham comes down from the mountain of sacrifice alone. Abraham does not in this midrash kill Isaac, but he does sacrifice Isaac *for* God or *to* God. Abraham and Isaac make their own way separately home from the mountain, and never again is Isaac at ease with his father. Wiesel takes the passage seriously enough to be horrified by it, and to hear it on a human level.[60]

I hope I am not trivializing the horrific and magnificent story of Abraham and Isaac by finding in it a tug at my own parental heart, and I certainly do not mean to elevate our own small family story into something grand and epochal. All I mean to say is this: Your calling from God is your own. I did not really take you up this mountain, and your pilgrimage of faith is not a sub-journey of mine. God and the community of faith through whom you are discerning his call brought you to this mountain. I have just had the privilege of accompanying you to the summit.

When I got on the train, and as I exchanged waves of goodbye with you, as you grew smaller on the platform and I pulled away, I felt a distance open up between us I had never felt before. I felt somehow I had to let go then.

Maybe all of this is somehow connected. Maybe part of what it means that Abraham's faith was reckoned to him as righteousness is related to his letting go of Isaac, though I can't (I won't!) stop resisting this text. I do believe that letting go is the essence of faith. Anyway, I do believe this is true: Abraham came down from the mountain alone. So Wiesel tells us. And Isaac found his own way back home. And still to this day we pray to the God of Abraham, Isaac, and Jacob, the God and Father of our Lord Jesus Christ. And, still, perfect love casts out fear.

Dear Jessica,

I've had Abraham on my mind lately, as Jeremy can tell you if you talk to each other this week. The passage from Abraham's story that I'm thinking about as I sit down to write you today has to do with blessing. *You are blessed to be a blessing.* That's what God told Abraham, and the same holds true for us all. This is why I think that stewardship is at the core of human life — generosity of spirit and purse toward others, and caring for the world in which we live.

If I were going to translate this spiritual teaching into the vernacular, I might say simply, "Tip extravagantly." This isn't just because most of the people who work for tips are among the most economically vulnerable people in our society — though that isn't a bad reason — it's because there's something in the nature of tipping extravagantly that smacks of the character of God.

Paul Scherer, a remarkable teacher and writer of an earlier generation, once wrote a book of meditations titled *Love Is a Spendthrift,* in which he says: "Love is a spendthrift, leaves its arithmetic at home, is always 'in the red.' And God is love."[61]

I think I have learned more about generosity from you, Jeremy, and your mother than from anyone else I've known: the way Jeremy, even when he has little money in his pocket, makes sure to tip a waiter or waitress generously; the fact that your favorite Christmas season activity is giving to the Heifer Project and the Salvation Army and Toys for Tots; or your mother's idea of keeping granola bars and fruit in the car so she can give them to homeless people panhandling at street corners. Her view is that while testing other people's means and motives might be sensible government policy, it is not permitted for followers of Jesus. (Jesus, according to your mother, is very disruptive to sensible government policies!) On top of that, you all work hard to challenge and change the social structures that support education, housing, and welfare. I know you see all these as "merely" human responsibilities rather than Christian ones, but I believe there's something more going on. I believe that when we are generous, we express the character of God revealed in Jesus of Nazareth.

Last year we had a luncheon to honor a former chair of our board of trustees. Several members of his family spoke, including his daughter. She related something that had happened that very morning as they were driving. Having forgotten to fill the tank before leaving Houston, they ran out of gas partway to Austin. A phone call later, a young man from a gas station in the next town found them, got them enough gasoline to get to the filling station, followed them there, and filled up their car. After the bill was settled the man handed his daughter two fifty dollar bills to give the young man. She said, "Daddy, I'm sure he would be more than happy with one of those." He said, "I don't want him to be happy. I want him to be ecstatic!"

Whether we are expressing our gratitude toward someone who has helped us or helping someone in need, whether extending care to an individual or developing structures of economic support to provide a more just society, whenever we act generously, in big ways or in small, we are reflecting the life and spirit of the God who throws lavish parties for prodigals and pays ridiculously high wages for short hours. I know this might sound strange to some folks, but I believe the meaning of life is being a good steward, which is another way of saying that the meaning of life can only be expressed in words like gratitude and generosity.

W. B. Yeats ends his poem "A Dialogue of Self and Soul" with the words, "We are blest by everything, / Everything we look upon is blest." We're called to live in this sort of moral posture, "blessed to be a blessing." We're not meant to understand Christian faith as an inquisition into the faults and failings of our neighbors, nor interpret the gospel of Jesus Christ as a conditional contract intended to exclude others, nor to see the way of God as an imperial victory march over the backs of those who differ from us. Rather, I think we're to see it as a lifelong expression of gratitude toward God that takes the form of generosity toward others. When I think of the phrase "meaning of life," this is what I think of more than anything else — not a tally of philosophical propositions, but a way of embracing life as a gift that can only be enjoyed through being given away.

So do we make meaning for ourselves, or is the meaning of life given to us? Both, I think, though the latter gives rise to the former. We make meaning of that which is given its meaning by the meaning-making God. (A philosopher would surely shake his head at that tautological merry-go-round!)

Let me take a more explicitly theological run at it. The theologian Jürgen Moltmann once noted that "Nietzsche was right in claiming that pagan religions were essentially festal religions." Moltmann does not dismiss paganism because of this insight; rather, he praises it. "In the feast, the finite and the limited human life is given the highest, because freest, expression before the infinity of the gods' world."[62] His insight, I think, takes us to the mystery at the core of Christian worship because *it is also at the heart of human life.* The act which forms the hinge of worship for Christians is the Eucharistic prayer, the great prayer of thanksgiving that precedes Holy Communion, an act that ritually remembers and spiritually resonates with our union with God in Christ, that act in which we are caught up into the eternal generosity of God and respond in gratitude. When we "lift up our hearts" in thanksgiving, we recall all that God has done and is doing and will do for us, we give God praise and thanksgiving, and we pledge ourselves to live gratefully. All of human life is raised up in a moment of feast, freely, joyfully, and the most ordinary, mundane aspects of human life are expressed "before the infinity" of God's world, a "world without end."

It seems to me that this insight from Nietzsche via Moltmann is all the more true because (and not despite the fact that) it reflects paganism and not just the Judeo-Christian traditions. Doesn't it make sense that the God who is bigger than any single creed has not been silent out there among the other peoples of the world and that what is true for a single faith is resonant with others? I think we can say this without being guilty of reducing the differences of faith to a false unity. A pagan can be as grateful and generous as a Christian or a Muslim or a Jew, and her gratitude and generosity can reflect the God who gives life to us all, because all are *blessed to be a blessing.*

Even the libertine antihero of *Les Liaisons Dangereuses,* who acts charitably just to try to impress and seduce a beautiful and virtuous woman — and is ultimately seduced by God into virtue and self-sacrifice — bears testimony to the power of the web cast by generosity. "I was astonished," he says, "at the pleasure to be derived from doing good, and I am now tempted to think that what we call virtuous people have less claim to merit than we are led to believe."[63] The joy derived from generosity and goodness is only strange if we assume that virtue must inevitably accompany mournful piety; but if goodness and joy come from the same divine root, doesn't it make sense that a joyful life and a self-giving life are synonymous?

Dear Jeremy,

Your comments about how beautiful the seminary campus is in the summer brought back a flood of memories of my own arrival at seminary. I also arrived in the summer, of course, though summer in Fort Worth, Texas, is very different from summer in Princeton, New Jersey.

As I think back thirty years ago, I still remember the excitement I felt beginning seminary. Some mornings I would get up early just to walk around the campus before anyone else was stirring. I thought of this today, actually, as I stepped onto our campus with the first blush of dawn just tinting the sky. Back then I felt like a kid who couldn't wait for the bakery shop to open so I could get the first hot rolls from the oven.

Some of my friends warned me that seminary would be the death of my faith. One wisecracker even called it the "theological cemetery." I confess I never, ever felt even remotely that way about theological education. Seminary, like college, opened to me the doors on a world of knowledge and wisdom I had scarce imagined before. I never feared it, and I never regretted it. Seminary invited me to explore sacred texts and ancient stories and rich traditions I had only superficially understood until then. The critical tools seminary gave me were a gift, and seminary gave me far, far more than it took away.

Knowledge isn't the enemy of Christian faith. Hatred, bigotry, small-mindedness, pride, and self-righteousness: all these are enemies of faith, but knowledge is not. If a class like Introduction to Old Testament threatens your hold on God's eternal covenant, it isn't just the walls of Jericho that need to fall. You already know this. You've always been a sponge soaking up everything you could learn, and you'll do the same in seminary. I remember how much you enjoyed your courses in Islamic studies and feminist theory in college. For you the question has never been, "Do I have to read all of this?" No, your questions have been "What is the best order to read this to get the most out of it?" and "When I finish these books could you help me figure out what to read next?"

I've been thinking recently about whether there's some message I should give you at the beginning of your seminary career that might help you focus on what's most important in your preparation for ministry. There is, and this is it: If seminary works the way it should, you will find yourself flatfooted in the presence of the awesome, stunning, overwhelming reality of what one of my professors once called GWAOT: *God, the World, and All Other Things.*

Some people run as fast and as far as they possibly can from the mystery and complexity of it all. They try to convince themselves that it is a virtue, a mark of faith, to remain ignorant. But no matter what anyone says, it's not a virtue; it's just cowardly and lazy. Other people run as fast as they can into the complexity, digging deeper and deeper into the details, sometimes becoming fascinated with the most minute and mundane of questions that demand years of painstaking work, and often no one else in the world cares about the answers they eventually discover. Usually these folks become Ph.D. students. Some emerge years later again as normal human beings with a lot of information. Some never quite make it out again.

Still others see in the overwhelming reality of mystery and

wonder a cosmic portrait that keeps them in proportion. The universe *is* unimaginably huge, and God is even bigger. We are very, very small, but by the grace of God and for reasons I cannot imagine, we are significant to God.

If seminary works well for you, you will find yourself standing in the presence of the mystery of life and (ultimately) the mystery of God. What you do with that experience is entirely up to you! Marcel Proust once said, "Since we are children who play with divine forces without shuddering before their mystery, we only find the telephone 'convenient,' or rather, as we are spoilt children, we find that 'it isn't convenient,' [and] we fill [the newspaper] with our complaints."[64] I fear that Proust's words hit my generation — the baby-booming "Me Generation" — especially hard.

We take the mysteries of existence and the wonders of God for granted, and spend an astonishing amount of our energy complaining that the plane is thirty minutes late when the marvel is that human beings can fly. I want to warn you against the sin of taking God's world and God and the wonders and graces (small and large) of your life for granted. To be grateful is just about the least we can do in the face of existence, and to be ungrateful is not only a sin, it's just plain tacky.

There is an alternative, however. One can stand before the mystery of life and of God, one can look up into the night sky and see the whirling, spinning majesty of the starry universe, and one can apprehend the worlds as God's playthings; and standing there, baptized in the exuberance of the universe and the possibilities of God, one can listen for a heartbeat beyond the clutter of all the background noise.

My late friend David Cairns once told me about how his father came to embrace the universe and God as good. It was an uphill battle. His father, D. S. Cairns, was principal of Christ College, Aberdeen. Principal Cairns lost his beloved wife to illness and raised their children alone. He was bereft and devastated by her death. He struggled with his faith for years. You can sense this in his book *The Faith that Rebels.*[65] But he also wrote *The Riddle of the World,* toward the end of which he says, "But the soul of Hebrew religion in its noblest manifestation in the prophets asserts this kinship in all those utterances of faith which assert the righteousness and grace of God. To assert these is to carry human values into the very heart of the universe, to proclaim that 'That which sits dark at the centre' behind Orion and the Pleiades and the Bear, that Sovereign Dweller in the Innermost is deeply akin to [humanity] and can be known and worshipped by [us], not merely because of His awful might but because, judged [even] by the standards of [humanity] He is just and good."[66]

At the core of the universe, there beats a human heart: the heart of God.

Son, I've made something of a career of denying the value of essentialism, the notion that the rich and varied complexities of life can somehow be boiled down to just one or two or three essential qualities. But I want to contradict myself now, at least in one regard. Throughout the Bible there are these moments when the clutter of codes and stories and prophecies gives way to a startling insight, a pure, happy moment of clarity and simplicity. Like the scientists who isolate and remove the background clutter that keeps us from hearing the heartbeat of the universe, some few prophets help us through the mass of details to hear the essentials. St. Paul writes: "But now abide faith, hope, and love, these three; but the greatest of these is love." St. James says: "Faith without works is dead." Micah asks: "What does the Lord require of you but to do justice, and to love mercy, and to walk

114

humbly with your God?" Jesus of Nazareth tells us: "Do unto others as you would have them do unto you."

As you begin seminary, I pray that you will embrace the complexity, but never lose the simplicity.

William Baer, the poet, says it like this in his poem, "Job."

Yes: wisdom begins with fear of the Lord,
which comprehends the power that made the seas,
the earth, the shimmering dawn, the unexplored
unfathomed skies, the moon, and the Pleiades,
which also know Who comes to judge our shoddy
little failing lives, knowing full well,
we need not fear the one who kills the body,
but only He who condemns the soul to hell,
which also knows it magnifies the Lord,
defying the demon, being the only release,
oddly enough, from fear, being its own reward,
which is also wise, is faith, is hope, is peace,
is tender mercy, over and over again,
until, at last, is love, is love. Amen.[67]

As you begin seminary, son, I would not want you to neglect your studies. I hope you bring to every task of your preparation for ministry both the seriousness and the imaginative play that becomes the high calling to which you are called. And I hope that you will enjoy the deep, rich, abiding complexities of theology and biblical studies that have challenged the brightest and best minds of the centuries. But I pray, too, that you will not forget the simple message of another poet, Philip Larkin, that sad old Anglican agnostic I admire, who once said, "What will survive of us is love."[68]

Dear Jessica,

I know of no great soul who has not passed through the wilderness, a desert place where he or she was tested, often under the blistering glare of the most terrible loneliness. Great saints of the early church, like Anthony, fled to the desert in imitation of Jesus. I suspect St. Anthony, the greatest of the early Christian hermits, went a bit mad in the wilderness, but perhaps we all go a little crazy on the way to sanity.

Jesus, of course, was driven by God's Spirit out into the wilderness, where Satan tested him with power, fame, and glory — the story is in Matthew 4. In Jim Crace's novel about Jesus' wilderness experience, one finds a God who is in the wilderness spaces between the words of the sacred text and metaphorically goes "to the very edges of the page," who dwells supremely in mystery, and refuses to come running obediently at our command, even if the one calling him is Jesus.[69] I find comfort, not least as a writer, believing that God goes with us to the edges of the page. I've spent a lot of my life beyond the margins that are justified — and, probably, justifiable!

Everyone who grows in wisdom, everyone who matures, everyone who learns to live well and truly and humanly passes through the wilderness on the way, and finds in the wilderness that which one must believe about God and oneself. The wilderness is, by definition, a hard place and a lonely place.

When you called me the other night, I sensed that you were in a wilderness.

Maybe it helps to know that others have been there too. When I read Dante's *Divine Comedy* for the first time, reading those words, "Midway in our life's journey, I went astray from the straight road and woke to find myself alone in a dark wood," my wilderness became just a little less bleak knowing the poet had been there before me.[70]

But nothing entirely alleviates the pain of the wilderness, except to come through it, and to grow.

One of the bleakest wilderness experiences through which I have passed began in the months immediately following our arrival in Scotland in 1987. Although by every external indicator I should have been very happy — accompanied on an exciting adventure by a wonderful wife and young family, accepted into an excellent Ph.D. program under a caring faculty tutor, serving a historic congregation with an esteemed colleague — nevertheless I struggled with a profound loss of personal faith that I kept hidden from public view. I knew I was not, but I felt friendless. In fact, I had never before *felt* so alone in the universe, at least the universe inside my soul, as I sorted out the meaning of my life. I remembered then the words of one of my professors in college who, during an earlier struggle of faith, had said to me in his distinctive West Texas drawl, "Brother Jinkins, finally, you are standing naked all alone in the road before God. It's just you and God. Now, what do you believe?"

At the end of that profound spiritual disorientation, I realized that the whole painful wilderness experience of doubt was necessary, that I would not have grown had I not outgrown my previous theological understandings. The wilderness is the place where we are moved beyond the old and familiar into new ways of thinking and believing and living. But just to say that the wilderness is ultimately good and that we must pass through the wilderness (perhaps several times) does not make it easy.

You and Jeremy have both passed through your own versions of wilderness, and I would venture to say you will pass through many more.

There is, finally, one thing more I feel compelled to say about the experience of wilderness, and it is that nothing you find in the wilderness can separate you from God's love. Perhaps it takes the overabundance of light in the desert for us to see ourselves. Perhaps it is because the desert exiles all distractions that we can hear God.

Dear Jeremy,

Yesterday I received a letter from a young minister. He said he loves being a pastor, but he is struggling to find his way through a long and bitter church conflict. Meanwhile, he said, a variety of routine pastoral crises keep nipping like Chihuahuas at his heels. And, in the midst of all of this, he and his young wife are coping with the wondrous and life-changing event of the arrival of their first baby. He said that his life has become so off-kilter that he has almost completely lost the joy he knew when he entered the ministry.

Learning to live a balanced life is never easy, and even joyful events can sometimes contribute to life's crises. But finding balance in the life of ministry — and this includes the preparation for ministry — is one of the greatest challenges of this vocation you are entering. John Calvin was right about this (as he was right about so many things): ultimately it is our calling that sustains us in ministry. But sometimes it is hard to sort through the accumulation of life's debris, the flotsam and jetsam that move with every new tide.

In a conversation with you recently I referred in passing to Seneca's *Letters from a Stoic*. I'm reading them now, and I am deeply impressed with Seneca's wisdom. There is such sensitivity and humanity in his letters.

Too often, it seems to me, Christians fail to treasure the fact that we are human. I just got a copy, incidentally, of a new book by South African theologian John W. de Gruchy titled *Confessions of a Christian Humanist*. I've admired de Gruchy's work, especially on Bonhoeffer, for many years. I've just started reading it, but already in the prologue I'm resonating with his attempt to retrieve the classic term *Christian humanism*.[71] You knew I'd like that, didn't you? Perhaps it was Bonhoeffer's influence that brought both de Gruchy and me to the same place. We'll see as the book unfolds (I'll get you a copy of the book too).

Maybe the reason we lose our balance in the first place is related to the fact that we under-appreciate our humanity, that we as Christians forget that we are human. We treat our bodies with contempt. We ignore our limitations. We indulge in the self-destructive myth of our own indispensability. And we violate the sacred principle of Sabbath. Then we go to our physicians or our therapists or our pharmacists asking them to calm the symptoms of the illnesses we have induced, without any intention of dealing with the underlying causes.

But to get back to Seneca: I am struck by his sanity and clarity of thought, but most of all by his humanity. Like a good doctor he observes our actions in order to diagnose the root causes of our ills. The letter from Seneca to a friend that I want to quote to you takes up two issues that may seem unrelated, but they are not: *friendship* and *the balanced life.*

Seneca writes, "There are certain people who tell any person they meet things that should only be confided to friends, unburdening themselves of whatever is on their minds into any ear they please. Others again are shy of confiding in their closest friends, and would not even let themselves, if they could help it, into the secrets they keep hidden deep down inside themselves. We should do neither. Trusting everyone is as much a fault as trusting no one." He continues: "Similarly, people who never relax and people who are invariably in a relaxed state merit your disapproval — the former as much as the latter. For a delight in bustling about is not industry — it is only the restless energy of a hunted mind. And the state of mind that looks on all activity as tiresome is not true repose, but a spineless inertia."[72]

Before I say anything about Seneca's advice, I want to say just a word to you about making use of non-Christian thinkers like Seneca.

Calvin begins his *Institutes of the Christian Religion* with these words: "Nearly all the wisdom we possess, that is to say, true and sound wisdom, consists of two parts: the knowledge of God and of ourselves," and this wisdom, true and sound, is "joined by many bonds."[73] Calvin effectively dismantles the wall between the sacred and the secular, between the religious and the profane, and thus he might be described as a Christian humanist. Calvin also believed that Jesus Christ shares his humanity with us, not his divine nature.

I know I've said this to you before, but God didn't go to all the trouble of becoming human in order to make us religious. God became human to make us fully and truly human. If you will remember this, you will bring great sanity to your own life and to the lives of those you serve as pastor.

I suppose I'm going the long way around the block to say that all wisdom, no matter what the source, is within bounds for Christians. There's a great deal to learn about life from people who do not share our Christian faith, people like Epictetus and Isaiah Berlin, Epicurus and Ludwig Wittgenstein, and, in this case, Seneca.

It is a wonderful discipline not only for pastors but for all Christians to read the Bible every year, cover to cover. It is enlightening to use different translations each time you reread the Bible. I am constantly amazed at the new insights that emerge and the surprises that meet me in passages I thought I had exhausted long ago. I may have been exhausted, but the Bible never is.

But each year, as you already know, I also make it a point to reread the Epic of Gilgamesh and the *Tao Te Ching* because I respect the wisdom found in each. I love to read Rumi for the same reasons I love to read Thomas Merton. As a minister, as a Christian, as a human being, I want to connect with the deep streams of our common humanity. Jesus Christ is not only Lord of the Church; Jesus Christ is Lord of all creation. The Word through whom all creation was brought into existence speaks still through all of life. Thus wisdom, "sound and true," is sound and true wherever we find it, because all wisdom originates in God.

So, although he is not a Christian, I return to what Seneca says about living a balanced life because what he says is wise. He warns us to be attentive to the hidden compulsions that drive us. Or, to say it a bit differently, he tells us that the balanced life is a life liberated from such compulsions.

When I was in seminary, I went through Clinical Pastoral Education, or CPE. You'll hear more about CPE from your Committee on Preparation for Ministry. CPE was one of the most beneficial learning experiences of my whole life, though it was very difficult at the time. I encourage you to take CPE while you are in seminary. I still remember the intense emotional experience of our weekly interpersonal relationship seminars. These sessions were like nothing I had ever experienced before. Members of our small group of seminarians would talk and listen to one another, unwrapping our life experiences, our struggles with identity, vocation, and family. The whole experience was, as they say, like peeling an onion: layer by layer, with lots of tears.

Again, I found this experience very difficult. I came from a family (as you well know) in which we studiously avoided facing a lot of the things that really motivate and drive us, and I was very defensive about examining myself at these levels. I think I was afraid that if people knew my real motivations (maybe I was afraid if *I* knew my real motives) then I would somehow become unacceptable to them. Yet it was not until I came to believe that God's grace is stronger than my *dis*-grace that I could face the deep forces that shaped and motivated me. Of course, until I could face these forces, these compulsions and motivations, I was pretty much at their mercy.

I learned in CPE that the success of my theological education depended on the success of an even more basic *human* education, the education which Kierkegaard describes as the curriculum a person "goes through in order to catch up with himself." Anyone, Kierkegaard writes, "who will not go through this course [of study] is not much helped by being born in the most enlightened age."[74]

The compulsions that lead us to talk when we should be silent and to be silent when we should speak, the compulsions that drive us to inappropriate actions and inappropriate inaction can only be dealt with when we find the courage to name them. I was unable to find the courage to name these compulsions and to deal with them until I knew (really knew!) that there is nothing in the world that can separate us from the love of God.

The balanced life is a life liberated (or at least on the road to being liberated) from the unseen, unexamined compulsions and hidden forces that toss and turn us. Seneca understood the dangers of those inner forces and compulsions, although we have a real advantage over him in that we know something about God's grace that can liberate us from them.

Seneca also understood the importance of friendship for living a balanced life. C. S. Lewis in a letter to his friend Arthur Greeves called friendship "the greatest of worldly goods." Lewis told his friend, "Certainly to me [friendship] is the chief happiness of life. If I had to give a piece of advice to a young [person] about a place to live, I think I should say, 'sacrifice almost everything to live where you can be near your friends.'"[75]

Well, son, you may not always be able to live near your friends if you become a pastor; the pastoral calling can separate us geographically from those we love, as you already know. But you must not allow the pressures and busy-ness of life and work to steal those friendships from you. Friends keep us in balance. Friends keep us from taking ourselves too seriously. Often a friend's laughter is a signpost pointing to our own absurdity, turning the light of grace on a fault so we can correct it. A friend may be the only person who loves you enough to read your sermon manuscript for the next week and tell you: "I know how you feel; but you shouldn't say that in your sermon." Or, "I agree with you and I'd be angry too; but don't mail that letter." Or, "I understand why you feel the way you do; but for God's sake don't *do* this."

On the high wire of life and Christian ministry, there are times when the net below us is unsure and the wire on which we balance has become frayed. Sometimes the only thing that we have to steady ourselves is a friend's voice. The words may be spoken in reproof or in comfort. But if you know they are spoken in friendship, they may just save you from yourself.

Finally, and this is all I'm going to say on this subject for now, Seneca understood that manic activity is seldom productive, but a person (and this includes a pastor) who can't get to work on time will fail to inspire much confidence.

I think that's all I've got to say on the subject of the balanced life.

Dear Jeremy,

Okay. I was wrong. Upon reflection, I have something else to say about the balanced life. Actually, I think I need to balance my previous comments on balance, even at the risk of contradicting myself.

The life to which we are called in Jesus Christ is not necessarily a balanced life. The Christian life (and this extends to the life of Christian ministry) is, in a way, a profoundly *un*balanced life. The Christian life is not simply the life of moderation described by Seneca the Stoic. The Christian life is a life of holy excess — not fanaticism, but excess nonetheless.

Let me try to write myself out of the corner I painted myself into.

Reinhold Niebuhr, in the diary he kept as a young pastor, observed of himself: "I am not really a Christian. . . . I am too cautious to be a Christian. I can justify my caution, but so can the other fellow who is more cautious than I am. The whole Christian adventure is frustrated continually not so much by malice as by cowardice and reasonableness. . . . A reasonable person adjusts his moral goal somewhere between Christ and Aristotle, between an ethic of love and an ethic of moderation. I hope there is more of Christ than of Aristotle in my position. But I would not be too sure of it."[76]

Later in his diary Niebuhr says: "It is almost impossible to be sane and Christian at the same time, and on the whole I have been more sane than Christian. I have said what I believe, but in my creed the divine madness of a gospel of love is qualified by considerations of moderation which I have called Aristotelian, but which an unfriendly critic might call opportunistic."[77]

I have sometimes said half-jokingly that I like to read the Stoics, but I prefer to dine with the Epicureans. What is probably more accurate is that I live in a tension between the good life as defined by the ancient Greek philosophers and the call of Jesus Christ to take up my cross and follow him.

There is indeed something of a "divine madness" about the gospel of Jesus Christ. There is an outlandish, outrageous, insane extravagance about God's mercy that acts without reservation and without the expectation of getting anything in return. But it is precisely in this holy madness that God reveals his own humanity, and shares it with us.

Dear Jessica,

You know that I love you. I also want you to know that I am proud of you. (I recently told your brother precisely the opposite. He knows I am proud of him. I want him also to know that I love him.)

You have wrestled with independence: declaring it early — as soon as you graduated from high school and moved out of the house — and working at it hard — making starts at various jobs and schools and struggling to have financial independence. I have joked with you that you saw through academics much too early. The ideal time to see through the game of academics is after you get tenure as a professor. If you don't see through it by then you're just pitiful. But seeing the elements of a game is not the same thing as being prepared to play it. And you know this too. I am pleased that you have found at last an education you enjoy seeking for the sake of the knowledge, and that you are excited about a future with a business of your own. I have, as you know, always admired the courageous entrepreneurs who start their own businesses, and I have sometimes envied them. I love risk-taking, and you are a risk-taker. I am proud of you.

Here's the thing I want to say about independence. We humans are not really individuals, and individualism as a creed is largely a dead-end road. We are persons, and our humanity is realized in a matrix of relationships. We are called to our humanity by the God of covenant, and we are called into the fullness of human life by the terms of this covenant, unconditional in the claims of God's love that lays upon us an unconditional obligation of mutuality. We live for one another, and that's how we become ourselves.

I want you to be appropriately independent. I want you to make your way in this world, pay your bills, work hard, and be proud of your accomplishments. But part of being appropriately independent is receiving with grace what you need from others. This is just as true to your humanity as learning to give with generosity what others need from you.

There's no formula that infallibly guides us here. There are no answers in the back of the textbook to tell us how to do everything right. The desire of human beings to have some infallible code of conduct, some utterly reliable set of rules, unfailing laws, or intractable principles, in place of a living faith in the living God is, I believe, the original sin. We just don't have this (not even in the Ten Commandments, the Levitical Codes, or the Sermon on the Mount). We live in a web of mutuality. We live covenantally. We live in God in Christ. Our life is hidden in him. Does this freak you out as much as it does me?

I am proud of you because I love you.

Dear Jeremy,

"What should a person expect to get from seminary?" Good question. The answer I want to give you is meant for you, of course, but it could apply just as easily to any young person pursuing any form of higher education.

There are several things I hope you get from seminary. I hope that you will gain a feel for how the long quest to understand God more truly contributes to and gains from humanity's search for knowledge. This is something I wish every Christian had. Wherever we have been permitted to freely inquire into the mysteries and problems of life and death, to ask the big, intractable questions of existence and creation and the nature of all things, including the nature of God, faith has flourished. But wherever the search for knowledge has been disdainfully dismissed as "mere academics," or has been controlled by those who fear the implications of new ideas and new information, the life of faith itself has shrunk and the church has grown cultish and sectarian.

Too many Christians seem intent on protecting God from new ideas, and I don't think God needs or wants our protection. I pray that your theological education has the courage to embrace knowledge, all knowledge, with confidence.

I also hope that you will come to possess wisdom, with all that entails. I don't know if you remember this, but the motto of my university was *Initium sapientiae timor domini,* "The beginning of wisdom is the fear of God." (In contemporary language, we'd probably say "reverence" instead of "fear.") It is simply true that knowledge and wisdom are not the same things. I want you to be knowledgeable, but I hope even more for you to grow wise. Wisdom comes from reverence. Wisdom knows its own limitations because wisdom knows the God who is holy and wholly other, irreducible to human schemes, inhabiting an utterly different order of being, beyond all creaturely being. Yet this holy and wholly other God has, we believe, become flesh and dwelt among us, has become a human being just like us. If our faith hopes to do justice to the reality of God it must learn to love mystery, not just tolerate it. It must hold the tensions, the rich ambiguities of our beliefs, the contradictions, and it must do so with joy.

Your comments about certain classmates who are preoccupied with orthodoxy strike me as particularly perplexing in this context. Often it seems to me that some people use the word *orthodoxy* mostly to exclude the questions of others. When Henry Ward Beecher once wrote, "Orthodoxy is MY doxy; heterodoxy is YOUR doxy," he was lampooning an attitude that is no less persistent today than it was in his own nineteenth century.[78]

What so many people forget in their concern over possessing the "right" *(ortho)* beliefs is that the great orthodox creeds and confessions of the Church, like the Apostles', the Nicene, the Westminster, and so forth, were written to preserve the mysteries of our faith from reductionism, to hold the tensions in tension.

Remember: it was the conservative Arius, not the liberal Athanasius, who threatened fourth-century Christianity's faith. Arius, piously defending the immutability of God (to put it bluntly, defending God against the dangers of creaturely existence, like change and decay) that could not reconcile the eternal being of God with the Incarnation. Athanasius, on the other hand, faced the startling, unprecedented problem of Jesus Christ with radical courage. Our understanding of God, according to Athanasius, needed revolutionary reinterpretation. And so the orthodox theologians, through a process of argument and negotiation and compromise that I believe speak of the Holy Spirit's continuing presence among frail humans, forged confessions that refused to reduce the reality of God's Incarnation to conceivable categories: "We believe in one Lord Jesus Christ, the only-begotten Son of God, begotten of the Father before all worlds, God of God, Light of Light, very God of very God, begotten, not made, being of one essence with the Father; by whom all things were made." All the orthodox did was to preserve the mystery of God's inconceivable acts among us.

What orthodoxy cannot mean is that Truth has been captured in a proposition — not if God is revealed in the flesh of Jesus Christ. G. K. Chesterton, the English journalist who wrote more beautifully and winsomely on the subject of orthodoxy than any theologian I've ever read, speaks of the "exact and perilous balance" required of us to live faithfully, a balance, he says, "like that of a desperate romance." A person of faith, Chesterton seems to say, should be possessed of the simple sanity that, because it is sane, is also mystical. He calls this person "the ordinary man" who "has permitted the twilight." "He has always left himself free to doubt his gods; but . . . free also to believe in them. He has always cared more for truth than for consistency. If he saw two truths that seemed to contradict each other, he would take the two truths and the contradiction along with them. . . . It is exactly this balance of apparent contradictions that has been the whole buoyancy of the healthy man. The whole secret of mysticism is this; that man can understand everything by the help of what he does not understand."[79] (And this warm praise of mysticism was written, mind you, by the same fellow who even contradicted himself by saying that mysticism usually begins in "mist" and ends in "schism.")

Any orthodoxy (whether of the "right" or the "left") that thrives on limiting its utterances to that which is non-contradictory (or, as you'll soon learn the word I'll use it now, non-dialectical), that which can only be stated unequivocally, has excluded both God and humanity. The core task of orthodoxy is to preserve the irreducible mystery of God. It is to resist the manufacture of what Donald MacKinnon once described as Aaron's god, the idol "fashioned of precious materials, given freely, indeed most generously, by those who would have their god set forth before them in an object at once precious and made to measure."[80]

Never forget: God's ways are not our ways, not even our most virtuous ways, not even our most religious ways, not even our most clever ways. God's thoughts are higher by infinity than our thoughts. God's hopes live in an altogether different realm, far removed from mere human aspirations. We can never own, never control, never possess God. But we can possess a measure of wisdom. And the wisdom, the deep wisdom, we are called to possess begins in the even deeper reticence of the creature before the Creator, "Immortal, Invisible, God only Wise."

Over against a religious culture that seems to think that piety means equating the mind of God with our position *du jour,* theological education at its best never strays from the humble acknowledgement that God alone is God, that every human word about God (and this includes theology) remains just that, a *human* word.

I was struck recently by what laypeople across the country told our seminary faculty. We sent out a survey asking what qualities they look for in a pastor. Do you know what they told us? They said they want "humility." They want pastors who can preach well and lead competently. But at the top of their list, they want pastors who aren't arrogant.

I also hope your seminary will give you an even larger perspective on what it means to be Christian. Even the most "churched" people (and you, as a "child of the manse," are about as churched as you can get) have a relatively narrow experience of Christian faith in contrast to the wide, wide, world of twenty centuries of Christian faith. From the beginning of your seminary career you will be given the opportunity to gain new perspectives on Christian life and ministry and practices of faith: new *theological* perspectives, new *historical* perspectives, new *philosophical* perspectives, and new *biblical* perspectives on every aspect of the life of faith. You will discover, for example, how one of the Church's earliest theologians, Origen, danced on the razor's edge of heresy, and how the risks he took made it possible for the Church to formulate the great confessions of our faith that have preserved the mystery of the Trinity. You will explore the strange fact that even the concept of "church" (which most of us take for granted) has had an astonishing variety of faithful forms across the centuries. You will delve into the biblical texts employing critical instruments while also listening for the Word of God speaking to you today.

Seminary is often the place where people discover for the first time in their lives that our love of God is never complete until we love God with our minds, as well as with our hearts and souls. I pray that your experience of God and of Christian faith grows ever larger.

And I hope that you will gain a richer, deeper, larger understanding of the life of the Spirit. You are so eager to grow spiritually. I see it every day in things you say and do, and I believe you are going to be a person of prayer and deep faith. My hope for you is that seminary provides you with a place where you can gain an even richer sense of God's Spirit.

You notice I am avoiding a particular word to describe what I hope you gain: the word that is so popular today, *spirituality.* The reason I am avoiding it isn't because it's a bad word. It's really a very good word. But popular culture has reduced this wonderful word to an individual matter of private feelings about the transcendent (whatever the transcendent may mean to you), and has placed it in opposition to the ordinary practices of prayer and worship in communities of faith.

From a biblical perspective, however, to speak of the life of the Spirit is to speak about God with us, and what it means for us to live together a life of integrity in relationship with God and others. Spirituality, from a biblical perspective, is public, grounded in corporate worship. It begins in the hearing of the Word of God and remains incomplete until it changes our behavior toward others. And, though many people even in the church have forgotten this, spirituality assumes that one's scholarship is as much a matter of faith as is prayer and scripture reading. This is crucial to remember in a time when pastors boast more of the fullness of their calendars than of their libraries. By the way, an editor at a leading publishing house recently told our faculty that pastors today read an average of only three books a year (and that includes recreational reading!). That was a depressing message.

Dear Jeremy and Jessica,

Not long after each of you was born, I sat down and wrote a short essay, a letter, addressed to you. I've mentioned this to you before. These letters are in the baby books that your mother lovingly assembled to record the various landmarks of your childhoods. Recently I read these essays for the first time since I wrote them. Jeremy's was a reflection on baptism and God's unconditional acceptance of us before we can make any claim on God; Jessica's an affirmation of the fundamental goodness of God's creation. Both were about beginnings, covenants yet to be fulfilled, and promises yet to be kept.

Writing this book of letters to you over the course of more than a year, most of the time I have simply been so wrapped up in communicating with you that I haven't thought about where the book would end. But recently I have sensed the oddness of compiling letters in the midst of lives in full flow, and the fact that at some point this book must end even as our lives, by the grace of God, continue.

C. S. Lewis, when he wrote his diary of personal sorrow after his wife's death, *A Grief Observed,* set the boundary of that book artificially, but artfully, by filling up the notebooks he had on hand with his reflections in longhand. When these notebooks were filled up, he didn't go out to a stationery shop to buy more; he just stopped writing.

I am ending this collection no less arbitrarily, just as each of you begins a new chapter in your lives, a chapter marked by your pursuit of the education you need to pursue your vocation. It is not unique for true stories to be written this way. The Book of Acts has no conclusion. The life of God's Spirit continues to pen its chapters in the history of the Church. But just because a book has no formal conclusion does not mean that it has nothing to say about the end. I am, therefore, ending this book by reflecting on your future, our future, as human beings.

A few days ago, as I prepared to speak to yet another incoming class of seminarians, I was reflecting on a passage from Rumi, the thirteenth-century poet and mystic. You've heard me speak of him before. He writes, "With us, the name of everything is its outward appearance; with the Creator, the name of each thing is its inward reality. In the eye of Moses, the name of his rod was 'staff'; in the eye of the Creator, its name was 'dragon.' In brief, that which we are in the end is our real name with God."[81] Rumi's thoughts bring to mind the words of 1 John 3:2-3: "Dear friends, now we are children of God, and what we will be has not yet been made known. But we know that when he appears, we shall be like him, for we shall see him as he is. Everyone who has this hope in him purifies himself, just as he is pure."

You, Jeremy and Jessica, are my friends and my children, and though I do not know all that you shall become, I know the name by which you shall be called, because you are created in the image of that name and you shall be drawn inexorably into the full reality of that name when he appears. So I end this collection of letters with a prayer from Ephesians (3:14-21): "For this reason I kneel before the Father, from whom his whole family in heaven and on earth derives its name. I pray that out of his glorious riches he may strengthen you with power through his Spirit in your inner being, so that Christ may dwell in your hearts through faith. And I pray that you, being rooted and established in love, may have power, together with all the saints, to grasp how wide and long and high and deep is the love of Christ, and to know this love that surpasses knowledge — that you may be filled to the measure of all the fullness of God. Now to him who is able to do immeasurably more than all we ask or imagine, according to his power that is at work within us, to him be glory in the church and in Christ Jesus throughout all generations, for ever and ever! Amen."

In the same spirit in which I placed you, Jessica, in God's hands when long ago you were wheeled into an operating room to have your heart opened up by the hands of a surgeon; in the same spirit in which I placed you, Jeremy, only a few months ago in the hands of God when I left you on a platform in Princeton not knowing where your calling may lead, but taking seriously Bonhoeffer's sober words that whenever God calls us God bids us come and die; in this same spirit I now commend you both into God's hands, trusting that God is able to do in you immeasurably more than all I can ask or imagine.

Only by entrusting you and your future to God am I able to love you in the full freedom of your humanity. That doesn't mean I won't still bug you from time to time, but I'll try to keep it to a minimum.

Love,
Dad

Endnotes

NOTE TO WHY I WROTE THIS BOOK

1. W. Robert Connor, "The Right Time and Place for Big Questions," *Chronicle of Higher Education,* June 9, 2006, B8.

NOTES TO A LETTER TO EVERYONE ELSE

1. Blaise Pascal, *Pensées,* trans. A. J. Krailsheimer, rev. ed. (New York: Penguin, 1995), 122.
2. Comment by Marilynne Robinson at the Center of Theological Inquiry, Princeton, Luce Hall Conversation, "The Future of Theological Inquiry in the Academy, Church, and Media," April 19-21, 2007.
3. Hans Urs von Balthasar, *Credo: Meditations on the Apostles' Creed* (New York: Crossroad, 1990), 30.
4. Abraham Joshua Heschel, *Man Is Not Alone: A Philosophy of Religion* (New York: Farrar, Straus and Giroux, 1951), 59.
5. Søren Kierkegaard, *Attack Upon "Christendom,"* trans. Walter Lowrie (Princeton: Princeton University Press, 1944), 18-44.

1. Kurt Vonnegut, *God Bless You, Mr. Rosewater* (New York: Dial, 2006), 129.
2. Frederick Buechner, *Wishful Thinking: A Theological ABC* (New York: Harper & Row, 1973), 25.
3. George MacDonald, *The Princess and the Goblin and The Princess and Curdie* (Oxford: Oxford University Press, 1990), 121.
4. Cited in Stephen Mitchell, *Gilgamesh: A New English Translation* (New York: Free Press, 2004), 48.
5. Buechner, *Wishful Thinking*, 95.
6. Eberhard Busch, *Karl Barth: His Life from Letters and Autobiographical Texts* (Philadelphia: Fortress, 1976), 496.
7. Dietrich Bonhoeffer, *Discipleship,* trans. Barbara Green and Reinhard Krauss, ed. Geoffrey B. Kelly and John D. Godsey (Minneapolis: Fortress, 2001), 43, 45.
8. Robert Farrar Capon, *Exit 36: A Fictional Chronicle* (New York: Seabury, 1975), 106.
9. Capon, *Exit 36,* 132.
10. George MacLeod, *Only One Way Left* (Glasgow: The Iona Community, 1953), 35.
11. William Sloane Coffin, *Credo* (Louisville: Westminster John Knox, 2004), 59.
12. George MacLeod, *Only One Way Left,* 38.
13. Clarence Jordan, *The Substance of Faith and Other Cotton Patch Sermons,* ed. Dallas Lee (New York: Association Press, 1972), 42-43.
14. Carlyle Marney, *Priests to Each Other* (Valley Forge, Pa.: Judson Press, 1974), 71.
15. Albert Schweitzer, *The Quest of the Historical Jesus: A Critical Study of Its Progress from Reimarus to Wrede* (London: Adam and Charles Black, 1910), 401.
16. Pascal, *Pensées,* 74.
17. Dietrich Bonhoeffer, *Letters and Papers from Prison,* ed. Eberhard Bethge (New York: Macmillan, 1971), 381.

18. Donald E. Miller, *Reinventing American Protestantism: Christianity in the New Millennium* (Berkeley: University of California Press, 1997), 3.

19. Bonhoeffer, *Letters and Papers from Prison,* 382-83.

20. Bonhoeffer, *Letters and Papers from Prison,* 383.

21. John Calvin, "Catechism of the Church of Geneva," in *Calvin: Theological Treatises,* ed. J. K. S. Reid (Philadelphia: Westminster Press, 1954), 93.

22. Elie Wiesel, *Memoirs: All Rivers Run to the Sea* (Toronto: Alfred A. Knopf, 1994), 85.

23. "Confession of 1967," in *The Book of Confessions of The Presbyterian Church (U.S.A.),* The Constitution, Part 1 (Louisville: Office of the General Assembly of the Presbyterian Church [U.S.A.]).

24. Joseph Sittler, *Gravity and Grace: Reflections and Provocations* (Minneapolis: Augsburg, 1986), 34.

25. Lao Tzu, *Tao Te Ching,* trans. Gia-Fu Feng and Jane English (New York: Vintage, 1972), 31.

26. Both of these passage are cited in Elizabeth Saintsbury, *George MacDonald: A Short Life* (Edinburgh: Canongate, 1987), 138.

27. Robert Frost, "The Road Not Taken," in *The Poetry of Robert Frost,* ed. Edward Connery Lathem (New York: Holt, Rinehart and Winston, 1969), 105.

28. T. H. L. Parker, *John Calvin* (Tring, England: Lion, 1975), 63.

29. Bill Wylie Kellermann, ed., *A Keeper of the Word: Selected Writings of William Stringfellow* (Grand Rapids: Eerdmans, 1994), 71-72.

30. Harold S. Kushner, *When Bad Things Happen to Good People* (New York: Schocken, 1981), 6-7.

31. C. S. Lewis, *A Grief Observed* (New York: Seabury, 1961), 26.

32. Søren Kierkegaard, *A Kierkegaard Anthology,* ed. Robert Bretall (New York: Modern Library, 1946), 10.

33. Parker Palmer, *Let Your Life Speak: Listening for the Voice of Vocation* (San Francisco: Jossey-Bass, 2000), 1-8.

34. Owen Chadwick, cited in Larry Witham, *The Measure of God: Our*

Century-Long Struggle to Reconcile Science and Religion: The Story of the Gifford Lectures (San Francisco: HarperSanFrancisco, 2005), 2.

35. Isaiah Berlin, *The Magus of the North: J. G. Hamann and the Origins of Modern Irrationalism,* ed. Henry Hardy (London: John Murray, 1993), 40.

36. W. H. Auden, "For the Time Being: A Christmas Oratorio," *Collected Longer Poems* (New York: Random House, 1965), 138.

37. Paul Elie, *The Life You Save May Be Your Own: An American Pilgrimage* (New York: Farrar, Straus and Giroux, 2003), 81.

38. Heraclitus, *Fragments,* trans. Brooks Haxton (New York: Viking, 2001), 27.

39. Bernard McGinn, *The Mystical Thought of Meister Eckhart: The Man From Whom God Hid Nothing* (New York: Crossroad, 2001), 38.

40. Rumi, *The Rumi Collection,* ed. Kabir Helminski (Boston: Shambhala, 2005), 13.

41. A. N. Wilson, *C. S. Lewis: A Biography* (London: Collins, 1990), 213.

42. A. R. Vidler, ed., *Objections to Christian Belief* (Philadelphia: Lippincott, 1964), 8-9.

43. Karl Barth, *Dogmatics in Outline* (New York: Harper & Row, 1959), 59.

44. Robin Jenkins, *The Awakening of George Darroch* (Edinburgh: B. & W. Publishing, 1995), 97.

45. Annie Dillard, *Teaching a Stone to Talk* (New York: Harper & Row, 1988), 41.

46. C. S. Lewis, *Till We Have Faces: A Myth Retold* (Glasgow: Collins Fontana, 1956), 58.

47. Toni Morrison, *Beloved* (New York: Plume, 1988), 123.

48. Samuel Terrien, *The Elusive Presence* (New York: Harper & Row, 1978), 151.

49. Douglas Martin, "Rev. John Macquarrie, 87, Scottish Theologian, Dies," *The New York Times,* Sunday, June 3, 2007, 29.

50. John Macquarrie, *God-Talk: An Examination of the Language and Logic of Theology* (London: SCM Press, 1967), 246.

51. C. S. Lewis, *Surprised by Joy* (London: Collins, 1959), 184-85.

52. Michael Jinkins, ed., *John McLeod Campbell: Love Is of the Essence* (Edinburgh: St. Andrew Press, 1993), 36, 48-49.

53. Stephanie Dalley, ed. and trans., *Myths from Mesopotamia: Creation, the Flood, Gilgamesh, and Others* (Oxford: Oxford University Press, 1989), 103-109.

54. Charles Dickens, *A Christmas Carol,* in *Christmas Books: The Oxford Illustrated Dickens* (Oxford: Oxford University Press, 1987), 7.

55. Thomas Lynch, *The Undertaking: Life Studies from the Dismal Trade* (London: Vintage, 1998), 33.

56. Miguel de Unamuno, *The Agony of Christianity,* trans. Kurt F. Reinhardt (New York: Frederick Ungar, 1960), 32.

57. Emmanuel Levinas, "Time and the Other," in *The Levinas Reader,* ed. Séan Hand (Oxford: Blackwell, 1989), 41.

58. Louise Glück, "Brown Circle," in *Ararat* (New York: HarperCollins, 1990), 42-43.

59. Kierkegaard, *Anthology,* 118.

60. Elie Wiesel, *Messengers of God: Biblical Portraits and Legends,* trans. Marion Wiesel (New York: Pocket Books, 1977), 84-110.

61. Paul Scherer, *Love Is a Spendthrift* (New York: Harper, 1961), 15.

62. Jurgen Moltmann, *The Passion for Life: A Messianic Lifestyle,* trans. M. Douglas Meeks (Philadelphia: Fortress, 1978), 69.

63. Pierre Choderlos de Laclos, *Les Liaisons Dangereuses* (London: Penguin, 1961), 58.

64. Alain De Botton, *How Proust Can Change Your Life* (New York: Vintage, 1997), 161.

65. D. S. Cairns, *The Faith that Rebels: A Re-examination of the Miracles of Jesus* (London: SCM Press, 1928).

66. D. S. Cairns, *The Riddle of the World* (London: SCM Press, 1937), 325-26.

67. William Baer, "Job (Job 28:28)," in *Good Poems for Hard Times,* ed. Garrison Keillor (New York: Viking, 2005), 7.

68. Philip Larkin, "An Arundel Tomb," in *Philip Larkin: Collected Poems,* ed. Anthony Thwaite (London: Faber and Faber, 2003), 117.

69. Jim Crace, *Quarantine* (London: Penguin, 1997), 135, 137.

70. Dante, *The Inferno,* trans. John Ciardi (New York: Penguin, 1954), 28.

71. John W. de Gruchy, *Confessions of a Christian Humanist* (Minneapolis: Fortress, 2006).

72. Seneca, *Letters from a Stoic,* trans. Robin Campbell (London: The Folio Society, 2003), 5-6.

73. John Calvin, *Institutes of the Christian Religion,* ed. John T. McNeill, trans. Ford Lewis Battles (Philadelphia: Westminster, 1960), I.1.i, 35.

74. Søren Kierkegaard, *Fear and Trembling/Repetition,* ed. and trans. Howard V. Hong and Edna H. Hong (Princeton: Princeton University Press, 1983), 43.

75. C. S. Lewis, *The Letters of C. S. Lewis to Arthur Greeves,* ed. Walter Hooper (New York: Collier, 1986), 477.

76. Reinhold Niebuhr, *Leaves from the Notebook of a Tamed Cynic* (San Francisco: Harper & Row, 1956), 166-67.

77. Niebuhr, *Leaves from the Notebook of a Tamed Cynic,* 195-96.

78. Debby Applegate, *The Most Famous Man in America: The Biography of Henry Ward Beecher* (New York: Three Leaves Press/Doubleday, 2006), 248.

79. G. K. Chesterton, *Orthdoxy* (London: Bodley Head, 1908), 208, 47.

80. Donald MacKinnon, "The Inexpressibility of God," in *Themes in Theology: The Three-Fold Cord: Essays in Philosophy, Politics, and Theology* (Edinburgh: T. & T. Clark, 1987), 11.

81. Rumi, *The Rumi Collection,* 84-85.

Acknowledgments

I am grateful to those who read this book in manuscript, particularly my children, Jeremy and Jessica, each of whom responded to various letters and whose responses gave rise to subsequent letters. I am also grateful to Dr. Kay Bryant, a clinical psychologist and parent of two young adults, and to Ryan Pappan, a senior seminary student, for reading the manuscript and for providing their reflections and suggestions. Dr. Bryant brought her experience as a therapist and a parent to bear on these readings; and Ryan, best known through his popular and provocative blog, the Fettered Heart (http://www.thefetteredheart.com), offered extraordinary insights. I am grateful to Carrie Finch, my research assistant, for help with the indexing. As always I want to thank my assistant, Alison Riemersma, for help at every stage of the book's development. I want to thank Jon Pott for the invitation to write this book. Finally, I am grateful to my wife, Deborah, for her partnership in the adventure of parenthood.

Index

letting go, as, 101, 105-6; longing for God, as 14, 85; "negotiating all of life with God," as, 15; participation in the being of Jesus, as, 44, 127, 135-36; person (or people) of, 3, 10, 16, 41, 89-91; personal relationship with God, as 14-21, 23, 67-68, 92-93; public dimensions of, 9-13, 35-37, 44-47, 64-65, 107-10; purpose (end, goal, point) of, 9-16; questioning, vii, 67-73, 91-101; transformation, 45-46; trust (and confidence) in God, as, 3, 16-17, 19, 47-54, 61-63, 69, 90, 98-101, 128, 135-36

Farel, William, 57-58

Foote, Shelby, 102

Forgiveness, 27, 32-33, 53, 62, 79-81, 84

Franklin, Aretha, 100

Freedom, 3-7, 50-54, 102-6, 126-27, 136; "God loves freedom more than safety," 47-54; vocational choice and, 54-59

Friendship, 103-4, 117, 120, 123-24

Frost, Robert, 54, 56

Generosity, 107-10

Gilgamesh Epic, 94-95, 121

Glück, Louise, 103

God of Abraham, Isaac, and Jacob, 30, 83, 105-6; Creator, 4-5, 20-21, 37, 47- 54, 60-63, 68, 81, 87, 89-90, 99-101, 104-5, 121, 134-35; divine Lover, Beloved, Love, the, 78; existence of, 4, 14, 91; God and Father of our Lord Jesus Christ, 83, 106; incarnation of, 9, 30, 128-30; Father (Parent), Source, Almighty, 4-5, 17, 18, 33, 50-54, 60-63, 104-5; good, 3, 18, 49-54, 60-63, 89, 107-10, 113-15, 134; Holy Trinity, 83-84, 129-33; holiness (otherness, greatness) of, 20-21, 30, 32-33, 39, 41-42, 44-47, 48, 53-54, 60-63, 68-73, 83-88, 110, 112-15, 127-33; Living, the, 15, 20-21, 84, 127; names of, 27-33, 83-84; providence, 65; purpose of for our lives (meaning), vii, 7, 9-16, 17, 21-26, 65, 86, 89-91, 109-10, 120-21, 133-36; revealed in Jesus of Nazareth, 6, 30, 32-33, 45-47, 51-52, 62, 86-88, 92, 108, 125; suffering of, 51-52, 60-61

Goodness, 3, 10, 18, 62-63, 107-10, 134

Grace (God's mercy, unconditional acceptance, unmerited favor), 27-33, 40-41, 62-63, 79-81, 114-15, 122-23, 125; "cheap" vs. "costly," 28-29

Gratitude, 107-10, 113

147

148